ALLEN + JE SO-AFG-336 CLEY

I Remember

I Remember

Bonded Labor, Quicksand, and Good News
for Thousands

Das Maddimadugu's story, as told to Julia Guyer and Andrea
Buchanan, with other tales and reflections from a dozen friends

Das Maddimadugu

Compiled and Edited by
David Janzen

RESOURCE *Publications* · Eugene, Oregon

I REMEMBER
Bonded Labor, Quicksand, and Good News for Thousands

Copyright © 2012 David Janzen. All rights reserved. Except for brief quotations in critical publications or reviews, no part of this book may be reproduced in any manner without prior written permission from the publisher. Write: Permissions, Wipf and Stock Publishers, 199 W. 8th Ave., Suite 3, Eugene, OR 97401.

Resource Publications
An imprint of Wipf and Stock Publishers
199 W. 8th Ave., Suite 3
Eugene, OR 97401

www.wipfandstock.com

ISBN 13: 978-4-61097-868-2

Manufactured in the U.S.A

Contents

Contents

List of Contributors

Andrea Buchanan is a graduate of North Park University in Chicago, was an apprentice at Reba Place Fellowship in Evanston IL, and volunteered with Matilda Ministries for four months in 2009–2010.

Gerry Cooper was a member of the Taipei (Taiwan) International Church (TIC) Missions Committee and has coordinated a number of medical and dental mission trips from his congregation to India to assist Matilda schools, Bindu home children, and rural village pastors.

Julia Guyer is a graduate of North Park University in Chicago, was an apprentice at Reba Place Fellowship in Evanston IL, and volunteered with Matilda Ministries for four months in 2009–2010.

Don Jacobs was the Director of Mennonite Christian Leadership Foundation, established to encourage churches in the training and development of effective Christian leaders. The Annual Leadership Seminar that Das directed fit this description nicely.

Annie Janzen was head cook at the Canadian Mennonite Bible College in Winnipeg, Canada, for many years and there met Das and Doris in the late 1970's. She has traveled the world visiting her friends and now lives at the Bethel Place residence for retired persons. She enjoys gardening, cooking, and membership in the Grain of Wheat Congregation.

Joanne Janzen along with her husband David, are communal members of Reba Place Fellowship in Evanston, Illinois. They try to keep up with two children and their spouses, along with five grandchildren who live in New York, Pennsylvania, and Evanston.

Rev. P. Menno Joel is pastor of the Bethlehem Mennonite Brethren Church in Malakpet, Hyderabad. He is the former principal of the M. B. Bible Institute, academic dean of the M. B. Bible College in Shamshabad, and treasurer of the M.B. Church of India.

Noni Johnson came to India in 1995 as a nineteen-year-old volunteer from the Catskill Bruderhof. After rereading her letters to her family from that time away from home, she wrote these memories in October, 2010.

Larry Kehler befriended Das and Doris Maddimadugu in 1976 when they attended Canadian Mennonite Bible College in Winnipeg, Canada. Larry has been a pastor, a former editor of *The Mennonite*, and has served in many capacities with the Mennonite Church in the USA and Canada. Larry is a mission partner with the Maddimadugu's, regularly sharing their news with a network of friends in Canada.

Das Maddimadugu has narrated his life story beginning chapter 1.

Doris Maddimadugu tells her story in chapter 3.

Esther Maddimadugu is married to Brent Graber. They live in Elkhart, Indiana, where Esther regularly works in the Elkhart schools as a substitute teacher, still filling in where needed. She appreciates the diversity of her students. She is an excellent Indian cook and loves to share rice, curry, and chai with guests and friends.

Luke and Mary Martin were missionaries in Vietnam with Eastern Mennonite Missions where they met Das Maddimadugu in 1973. Luke worked for many years as a caseworker for Vietnamese clients at a social service center in Souderton, PA and has returned several times to Vietnam with tour groups.

Jeannie Stuckey and her husband, Dr. Allen Stuckey, live in Elkhart IN. They served with the Mennonite Central Committee in Vietnam from 1969 to 1972. Jeannie finds joy in sponsoring a Bindu Home child.

Introduction

JOANNE AND I FIRST met Das and Doris Maddimadugu one Sunday morning in 1975 when this dark-skinned couple appeared with their three-year-old daughter, at worship in New Creation Fellowship, an intentional Christian community in Newton, Kansas where we were members. After the service, while our children played together, we learned that Das and Doris had only weeks before, fled war-torn Vietnam in the last days of the Saigon regime, flying out with a plane load of orphans. Later, sitting on the floor in their apartment eating rice and curry with our unsteady fingers, we found kindred spirits—radical disciples of Jesus, eager for community, with a Gandhian vision for peacemaking and social justice.

Our friendship grew in the following six months while they worked for the Mennonite Central Committee, administering the relief supplies warehouse in North Newton and speaking often in surrounding churches about their experiences in Vietnam. After their term of service with MCC they moved to Winnipeg, Manitoba, to attend Canadian Mennonite Bible College. Eventually they returned to India where Das and Doris led an urban Mennonite congregation for eight years. We kept in touch through Christmas letters and occasional birthday greetings.

We felt the mysterious touch of God on our lives in 1990, on a Winnipeg, Manitoba, street when we spied Das and Doris coming toward us. From different continents, we met again at the Mennonite World Conference. Hugs and excited sharing ensued as we cut conference sessions in order to catch up on years of personal news. There we heard Das share his dream: "For eight years I had been a Mennonite pastor in Hyderabad. But I feel a call to start something in the region where my roots are, among the untouchable people. I want to bring a message of liberation, salvation, and education to the poorest and most neglected people of Andhra Pradesh." Joanne and I agreed to join them in a mission partnership, sharing Das and Doris' letters with about a hundred of their friends in the United States. Reba Place Church, in Evanston IL, where had lived since 1984, agreed to take up this project so that donations could be channeled to their work in India.

In 2007 I was able to spend nine days with Das and Doris, sharing their food and their love for the many children who daily surround their lives. I wanted to see with my own eyes the fruit of our partnership with Das and Doris, and with their other friends around the world. On the scooter, holding onto Das, we visited local churches, the farm, and other projects of interest. Some of these excursions are reported in the following pages. During that visit the Spirit planted the idea in my mind that, one day, Das and Doris's story should be told in their own words for a wider audience, to the glory of God.

In November, 2009, two young women from Reba, Julia Guyer and Andrea Buchanan, flew to Hyderabad to volunteer four months of service, teaching in the Matilda School in Mallepalli, and interviewing Das and Doris to record their life stories. With great care and skill, Julia and Andrea interviewed, transcribed, and sensitively wove these stories and reflections together into the narratives of Das and Doris's lives. We have chosen to take Das's story as the "main line" in this book because the arc of transformation in his life is more dramatic and because his vivid memory has preserved so many stories of his and Doris's life and ministry together.

As you will read, Das carries the painful consciousness of his roots as an "untouchable," a child nearly sold into bonded labor which, for many, becomes a lifetime of debt slavery. But instead he was "adopted" by a single Mennonite missionary woman who taught him about Jesus' love and gave him an opportunity to discover his gifts for wide-ranging study, loyal friendship, community organizing, and dreaming how to bring hope to those at the bottom of society's heap. God has used the improbable transitions of Das and Doris's lives to weave together a network of friends in places like Korea, Taiwan, Shanghai, Winnipeg, New Haven, Chicago, and Newton, Kansas. And this network of friends has become an innovative partnership in Jesus' mission of embodied "good news to the poor."

For some time I struggled with how to tell this story of God's work to redeem Das from the pit of destitution, and through him, to touch thousands of outcast children and adults through partnerships with churches and individuals around the world. Then a memory came back to me of an evening in 2007 with Das, enjoying conversation and the cool breeze on the rooftop of the Bindu Home.

As night was falling Das pointed out over the landscape of scrubby semi-desert planes, rocky mountain outcroppings, to the twinkling lights coming on from countless villages scattered across the horizon. He told of bicycle visits to dozens of tribal hamlets where he and his evangelist friends shared stories of Jesus, where house churches were born, where night schools gave children hope, and housing projects provided some stability for formerly nomadic families. As Das talked we moved around the roof top, ducking under wash lines full of hand-laundered clothing from 130 Bindu Home children who, beneath us, were brushing their teeth and preparing for bed. It occurred to me that the story of Das's life could be the "wash line" and the memories of mission partners and friends from around the world could be the "laundry" hanging from the cord. The effect would be impressionistic, many colors of cloth, waving in the breeze, united by their connection to the main story of God's liberating power that calls into being a people of praise. So this is what we have done. As you read on, the main story line in Das's own words will be hung with testimonies, memories, and reflections from others who have shared in this emerging story of liberation. I have also inserted a few of Das's poems, taken from a 2000 publication titled, *I Was There: Poems and Other Writings by Das Maddimadugu*, compiled by Larry Kehler.

As I wrote in the preface to that collection of poems, "Das and Doris are examples of an emerging vision for missionary partnerships between churches in the developed countries and indigenous church planters around the world. For the cost of supporting one North American missionary family, thirty Indian Christians are engaged in bicycle evangelism, running schools, caring for orphans, training church leaders, and making friends for Jesus." India is a multi-ethnic society with a painful colonial legacy and a fierce struggle for independence. Outsiders, soliciting "conversions" is a crime and can incite violent mob reactions. In this setting, by the most humble means, God is moving to plant and renew the church, a church responsive to the needs of the poorest and most marginal.

These stories have "grown from the rocky soil of an oppressive stone-cutters colony, of schools begun in cow sheds, of children sold into slavery and redeemed, of a small farm run on Jubilee principles, of so much hardship and early death that human empathy is exhausted and only Jesus can bear the soul-crushing load. These stories connect us to believers in another land, partners with us in the Gospel, prophets of a God whose grace surprises in the most impossible circumstances and who never ceases to care."

David Janzen
Evanston, IL
October 2010

Chapter 1

Childhood: Destitution, Survival, and a Second Mother

Famine and a Trek to Guntur

I REMEMBER WHEN I was about seven, my parents were both still living and it was a time of starvation in our land. People were migrating to other parts of our state, Andhra Pradesh. I remember my father and mother taking the two of us, my brother and me, and we walked towards the south. Now I know that we were walking south, but at the time I did not know north, south, east, or west.

My father put me on his shoulder, and he carried me while my brother walked and carried our things. There was not much to carry. We walked and when we got to a town we would stay at a site outside of the town or village for the night. There was no transportation. There were quite a few other people also going south, where there was more food, and more progress. So we walked, walked, walked. It was a difficult time.

We ended up in a city called Guntur, which is only six hours by bus, but takes much longer if you walk. My father had a cousin from our village who had moved to Guntur; he gave us shelter outside the city. He sold hay for cattle. He would go to a big haystack and get some bundles, and then sell the bundles to people who owned cattle and other animals in the city. These people would use it to feed the oxen that pulled their carts which carried people to their destinations. My father's cousin said he could help, and my father was happy to find work. We were all together, and I remember that that was nice. I even made some friends.

I followed some older boys who took me to a freight train hauling coal; they would jump up onto the train and throw off thick slabs of coal. Sometimes the station master came and we would all run away. It was fun. I would come home with a coal face. But then it became known that we were stealing coal from the freight trains, which never had occurred to me. I told my father what we were throwing off the train. He said I had to stop this. I remember realizing that this was wrong, and I did not want to disappoint my parents. While my father worked with hay, my mother would try to keep our clothes clean and find food for us.

My mother would go to a local small restaurant and get some dumplings. We called them *idlis*. She would give them to my brother and me, and we ate. Later on I realized that they were stale, leftover dumplings; they were yesterday's dumplings. But even today, those were the best dumplings I ever had. They had a very nostalgic smell, a smell like garlic. We have eaten many places, expensive places and inexpensive places, and I have had Doris's cooking. But when I think about the smell of those dumplings, I want to eat them again. Of course I never had them again, because later I would always have the fresh ones. But I think the dough of the old dumplings is my favorite.

Julia Guyer and Andrea Buchanan

Volunteers on the Way to India

Julia Guyer with Andrea Buchanan: Journal

October 31, 2009: Two in the morning in the Delhi airport—yesterday we were in three continents. Still one more flight to Hyderabad! All airports seem aggressive and void of personality. When we have questions, we try to look for women to ask. They seem more approachable. Many of the men in the airports carry guns, and I don't trust anyone who has an automatic weapon.

Nearly everyone in this small seating area is asleep. There are two grade school-aged kids camped out together on the floor. The older sister seems protective of the younger brother, even in rest. Andrea is snoozing on the chair next to me, folded over like a wind-up dancer from the Nutcracker Suite.

Andrea imagined the space which we will rent when we get to Mallepalli. Our apartment is supposedly right outside the school where we will teach. She thought of a little cot, pictures of our families on the floor by our beds, books neatly stacked, a little work space for our projects and for work on lesson plans, pillows for seating, and our iron skillet over the stove. Perhaps we can get fabric for curtains. I brought my sewing kit. All of this seems silly, but thinking about the space helps me feel grounded. Routines, prayer, domestic work—unavoidable things in the four months that approach us. Experiences which can tether us to the familiar. Otherwise we might get lost, float away. But we have each other.

November 1: Driving to Mallepalli from Hyderabad was a mess. The guy who got us at the airport, Das's cousin, tried to show us around a bit, but I was pretty out of it. The actual ride was like being a passenger in a non-stop drag-race while also playing chicken with oncoming traffic. At one particularly scary moment, Andrea reached out for my hand and did not release it. I thought I might lose several fingers from gripping her hand for the duration of our three-hour drive. And we are not the hand-holding

type. But it seemed incredibly appropriate and necessary because at any moment we could draw our last breath. If I hadn't been so jet-lagged I might've screamed. But it was exhilarating.

When we arrived at our new place, we cleaned and tried to settle in. We are on the second floor of a small cement two-flat. I don't really know how to describe it. People don't live in structures like this in the States. There are two little storefronts downstairs. I think families live there, too. I don't know how they have room. We share the front room with two twin beds squeezed in. We have a door to the balcony and a window looking out onto the street. There are built-in shelves on the wall. With our colorful bedding and mosquito nets and the periwinkle blue wall, our room is cheerful and seems to match the ruckus floating up from the street.

November 2: The Maddimadugus invited Andrea and me to dinner; we will try to have dinner together once a week while we volunteer in their school and orphanage. And twice a week we will interview them.

Das and Doris live next to the school and above the Bindu children's home. It is a cheerful apartment, neatly organized. They share the space with their son Nathan, who runs the schools they planted, schools which now welcome about 1,500 children. There are pictures of their family on the wall. I look at their daughters, one of whom lives in the States, the other in Canada. I wonder if they are so different than their parents. We step into the living room, which has a couch, a couple of chairs, and a TV. The kitchen has a table which Doris has already set with a delicious meal of curried chicken, rice, and a curd salad. I find it tricky to eat with my fingers. The Indian people make it look so simple. With the fingers of their right hand they manage to form a little ball of food and rice, and simply plop it in their mouths. I'm always smearing it over my face and hands. But I'm game to keep trying.

Doris is shorter than us, standing at about 5'0". She always wears a sari. She told us that her daughter Esther once asked her to try wearing choorie dhar, the traditional Hyderabad tunic and pants. Esther had said that they were incredibly comfortable and that she would love them. Doris tried once and did not like them. Her hair is always in a knot on top of her head. She has trouble walking sometimes because of a pinched nerve in her leg. She has trouble seeing, and wears glasses. Das and Doris are both growing old, but they have met age and time with grace. She is particular about how things are cleaned, and about speaking with correct grammar. Both Doris and Das's English is excellent.

Devadoss, whom we always call "Das," is an interesting man. He's shorter than me by about a head. My guess is that he's only a little over five feet tall. He's round in the belly, but wears it well in comfortable loose clothes in the western style. And he's extremely soft spoken, more so in English, I think, than in his native Telugu. His eyes water frequently from problems with cataracts, which his father also suffered from and which eventually caused blindness. He wears glasses with plastic aviator-type frames, which he removes when we are in conversation as if they are a distraction or discomfort. His face is long and rotund. His tidy beard and mustache have turned almost completely white along with his hair. It stands out impressively against his dark skin, darker around his eyes and across his cheeks. His face looks surprisingly smooth, there are no deep creases typical of aging. His wide lips frequently break open into a smile that is both friendly and respectful.

Das is full of welcome. Immediately I have been struck by an air of kindness about him which seems to linger in spirit after his physical presence is gone. For a man of his age, he has retained a sweetness and simplicity which is unusual to a person of his accomplishments. In his stillness I feel a deep current of wisdom that could easily pass by overlooked. Of all the men I've met in India, which is not that many, he is the most comfortable with us. He does not try to impress or seem to want anything from us. Rather, we are here, wanting something from him—his story.

When we met to interview him the first time, we entered his office, which was about six by eight feet and completely concrete, as most structures in India are (to withstand the elements). We sat comfortably in the cool shaded room, on plastic lawn chairs. There is one metal shelf along the wall, a metal desk, a sewing machine, several Bibles, and a calendar which also advertises the schools of their Matilda Education Society. We did not know how to begin, how to approach him about telling us his life story. How do you ask a person that? A dozen possibilities entered my head. All of them seemed inappropriate. I didn't want to throw him off by casually saying "spill it."

So we sat there patiently talking about the weather, how we were adjusting, and the ant bites Andrea was suffering from. By then Doris had joined us, and she told us about a chalk that we could buy at one of the bodegas which was good for killing ants and cockroaches. And she warned us that we needed to be very clean.

The conversation seemed slow and easy, so when Das asked us, "Well, what should I say?" we said, "We were hoping you could tell us about your childhood." In the straight-forward and unsentimental way that Das tells stories, he began.

Andrea Buchanan is a graduate of North Park University in Chicago, was an apprentice at Reba Place Fellowship in Evanston IL, and volunteered with Matilda Ministries for four months in 2009–2010.

Julia Guyer is also a graduate of North Park University in Chicago, was an apprentice at Reba Place Fellowship in Evanston IL, and volunteered with Matilda Ministries for four months in 2009–2010.

Mother's Illness and Death

My mother became very sick, and we returned to Devarakonda. We learned that she had chronic tuberculosis. An American missionary lady took her in. She put her in a room that was about 8 by 8 feet, and I took care of her. My mother was coughing, coughing, coughing all the time. And then this spit would come—thick, yellowish spit. It would have lots of germs. Later, when I became a medical lab technician, and I would test the spit of people, I would immediately recognize that this person has tuberculosis because my mother had the same kind of spit. Somebody who was with the missionary lady would feed both of us. She was very kind, though I don't know why. We were not there long, and we soon went home. The lady said that my mother could not be cured. I saw them bring a cart to the hospital. They took both of us with her pots and the things that she needed, and we went to my mother's native village of Chinthakuntla.

My mother had no one there except for one aunt in my mother's father's house. They lodged us there. They gave her a cot and we stayed, but she was always coughing. As soon as she coughed I would take a pan and put it by her mouth so she could spit into it. Sometimes I noticed that the yellowish color turned red with blood.

One day I went out just for a little while. When I came home I saw my mother signaling to me from her cot. She made a forwarding motion with her hand and called me to her. I didn't know what to do, and for some reason I didn't want to go to her, but I did approach her. She took my hand harshly. I would have been afraid if she were not my mother. It was strange how I felt a little bit afraid of her. So I went a little closer. She said still, "Come, come closer." I went very close to her and stood beside her. And she said, "You take care of yourself." I remember those words as she stretched out a hand to touch me, a very skinny hand—just skin and bones. So I clenched her hand and said, "OK." Then I went to touch her feet, and they were so cold. I asked her, "Why are your feet cold?" and she replied, "I don't know." When I asked her if I should cover her feet, she said, "Don't. No need."

The room was dark, no illumination. I was struggling there because, suddenly, I felt some kind of uneasiness, and I went out to find my aunt. I stood outside the door and called her, and then she came. She must have guessed what had happened. When we returned to my mother's room, she was still, and my auntie told me that she had died. She began to cry. I went out and told some of my relatives that my mother had died, and then they came. The only person that touched her though was this old lady, my aunt.

They sent word to my father and my brother. My father was in my home village and my brother had become a bonded laborer, working in a neighboring village. So he was on a farm somewhere, plowing, when our mother died. He was around thirteen years old, a very skinny boy at the time. When he heard that Mother died, he ran to the landlord and told him, and the landlord allowed him to come. Many people came. They gathered around in the front porch area and I was with my mother. My father and brother came, and we stood there to the side and cried for a while. They made a makeshift cart, and they carried her away. I followed. They carried her out from the village to some far place. It was around six o'clock in the evening, and they buried her there, in the dark. It had been a long day. I ate some food, and I slept.

Our family was small, only my father, my brother, the old lady-auntie, and me. My father left the next day and my brother left as well. The old lady and I remained. "You stay with me. You can help me with drawing water, getting firewood and doing things. And I will cook for you. I will make you good food." So I stayed with her. My brother went back to work for the landlord, and my father returned to the village.

Begging with My Father

Two weeks passed, and one day my father came to tell me, "I am going on to some villages to beg because I have no money now. This sharecrop won't give me any money. Do you want to come with me?" When I said "OK," we both left to beg. We would go to a known place, a village where we knew people. We would go to people with a reputation for having money. My father would stand in front of the house, and I would stand with him. They would ask him, "How are you? Where are you coming from? What happened?" So he told them, "My wife died, can you give something?" He would put his hand on my neck and say, "This fellow also needs something to eat," and they would give us food. When we had food, maybe from one or two families, we would sit outside the village by the well, draw some water, and eat our food.

Then word came that my aunt, my mother's sister, Shantamma, who lived in Hyderabad city, had come to our relatives in the village. She sent for us to return, which we did. My brother also came. She said, "This is no good way for children to live. I'll take you boys to a mission compound in Devarakonda. There you can read and write and learn. Would you like to?" I told her I would. When my aunt was young, she had studied at a missionary school up to grade seven. It was these same missionaries who had taken my mother in, and who then took me in to study.

I remembered the children who played around the mission compound where my mother had stayed when she was sick. Some of them were my friends, and they were going to school and some were children of employees of the hospital. I remember distinctly on Sundays that we would play a game called ding-dong. All the children would go and hide; one would search for them. The person who was out looking for them would have a little leaf, and when he would find someone, he would say "ding-dong" and give them the leaf. That person would be "it" and have to search the next time. The children would tease me because

I would hide in a place that I thought was secret. They would pretend that they could not find me, and then I would call softly "I'm here." They were very nice to me and it was fun, even when they teased me. I liked that a lot. I wanted to play with children, and I thought about that when I was heading to the mission compound; I thought it would be a magical place.

School, a New Mother, and a New Name

My aunt had brought clothes for me and my brother from Hyderabad. She paid the debt and retrieved him from bondage with help of the missionaries. She did not know our sizes, so the clothes were big, but I wore them to the mission compound. I didn't know what to expect, but my aunt had said "let's go to the garden," and I was imagining a garden with flowers and all kinds of trees. So the Sunday pastor accompanied us, and we entered the mission compound. We passed the big building, and I kept looking for a big garden. There was no garden. But there was a huge building with many shallow steps. We stood at the foot of the steps, and the pastor told us to fold our hands in front of us.

Then for the first time I saw the woman who would become like a mother to my brother and me. Helen Warkentin had been there for many years already. Her hair was a sandy blond color, and her eyes were an ocean blue. She was very dedicated and spoke perfect Telugu. My aunt pressed her hands together and bowed to her, like the traditional Indian greeting. Helen asked me what I and my brother were called, and then Pastor Samuel renamed us.

My name had been Yesu, and it was much abused in the village because when people called me they intoned a low-class utterance prefixing my name with 'ore'. My brother's name was Lingaiah. The pastor said that I was now "Devadoss." Deva means God, and Doss means servant. My brother's name was changed to Kupanandam, meaning the one who rejoices in mercy. My brother's name also meant joy and grace. Then and there, they gave new names for us. My auntie also approved of the names. We were told that we had to study very hard and behave ourselves.

They took us to a little hut with a thatched roof and one opening which was the entrance. There was no door, so I just walked in to my new home where there were, maybe, seventeen young boys living in one of several round houses. That remained our house while we were at the hostel. At night everyone would sleep on the floor. Each one had a box or trunk or some little bit of blanket, which we would wrap our clothes and books in. There were no mats. My brother was put in a different house which had older boys. We were separated by age and classes.

I was given a plate for eating the next afternoon. We all would stand in one place, girls in lines on this side, boys in lines on the other side. Our plates would already be there. We would all get food dished out of a big pot. And then we prayed:

> "Deva ma Bhojanambunu
> Deevinchi Maku Balamu
> Nosansu Matlu Cheyumu—Prardhinchachunavum—
> Amen."
> "Lord, thank you for this food, and as we eat this food, give us strength."

Three times a day, everyday, we would pray that prayer. A woman would stand by with a stick, and whenever anybody would move or open their eyes or go out of line, she would thwack them. We were very scared of her, but at the same time, she liked us. We knew that. We would take our food; I would always be with my brother. Sometimes the food was not much, and by the time we got our food, other boys were done with their meal. We would add salt to our water sometimes to help us feel full. My brother would fix my food for me, making it into a little lump. He always waited until I finished eating before he ate. Sometimes I would take his food on the sly, and he would never scold me. I would wash our plates and put them back. Because we were hungry we would drink so much water; we didn't even mind the salt.

We ate early and by seven or eight o'clock in the evening we would be hungry again. The children who had something to eat from their parents would eat snacks. We all liked snacks, but if we had nothing, we would sit and read. At anytime of the night, if someone woke me or any of the other boys were up and asked "would you like to have some food?" we would immediately sit up and say "yes." It would not matter if it was the middle of the night. If someone asked us if we wanted food, we would say "yes."

I Worked with the Buffalo

Helen wanted to know which children were ready to attend school. One of the first Sundays I was there, she came with an armload of books. She gave them to us while we sat in groups of four or five. They were English books and Telugu books. We weren't reading because we didn't know how, but we would identify pictures say the names of what we saw. Helen would observe us from a distance to see if we were reading or if we put the books aside to play. She would watch to see who had the potential to study well or not. So this is how she decided which of us were ready to go to school. Those who were not reading, who put their books aside and played with marbles, would care for the buffalo or tend the garden or something like that. But we all went to school sooner or later. For me and my brother, we had no parents to help pay for us, so we were required to do some work besides our studies. I worked with the buffalo.

I developed a routine at the hostel. In the early mornings I would go and help the buffalo man. We would take the buffalo down to the barn and the calves would follow. I would let the calf go to its mother before milking so that the calf would get the buffalo ready to give milk. That was the easy part for me. But pulling the calf back off its mother, while it used its full strength, that was hard. All the calf wanted was to drink right now, and sometimes the calf pulled me back with it. It became difficult to balance, and sometimes I would fall down. The ground was very slimy.

The old man who milked the buffalo would chide me, tease me, and say, "OK, OK, you are strong enough. Do that again." And of course I would fall down again. I had dung all over me, and he would always laugh. This was my first job. It was very early in the mornings, at four or five o'clock.

There were empty cans, and we would use these cans for carrying the milk. I was not very strong, and when I carried the milk I had to take my steps very, very gently so the can on my head would not tilt or spill. I had to go so slow until I reached the steps of the main house. Then the cook would come down and take the milk off my head and go inside. The cook would say "stay here," and I would stay. Then, he would come with a bigger load with liquid feed, put it on my head, and I would carry it all the way to the barn with the buffalo cows. I had to be very careful. The workers would not take the pack off of my head. They would tell me to put it down on my own, jokingly. Once in a while I would fall down while I was carrying the load because I had to keep my head straight and I could not see down, I could not see the stones. And then when I would fall they would laugh at me. That was fun for them, but not for me.

That was my work in the mornings and the evenings. But Sundays were the fun days. I and a boy named Jacob, with no mother or father, who had a limp leg, would take the buffalo to the lake and feed them for a while. Before bringing them back, we had to wash the buffalo in the lake and get them very clean. When we returned with the buffalo we would sit on them and they would run, run, run. Sometimes the buffalo would run through the trees and the bushes and we would laugh. Giving the buffalo a bath and taking a bath, that was fun. I always looked forward to Sunday because of this time with the buffaloes, because there was no school and not much work. We had no lunch, but still we enjoyed it.

Those were the early days. After doing this Sunday work for some time, I was told to go to Sunday school. I did not want to go. I insisted that Sundays were Buffalo Days. But Sunday school was where we learned Bible stories. We didn't have to stay for church, only the Sunday school. It turned out that, even after Sunday school, we would take the buffalos to the lake.

Stolen Lemons and a Snakebite

When the cattle had to rest and graze, they would stay in the hostel compound. On one side of the hostel there was an orchard, vegetable garden, and two lemon trees. I would sit on the wall of the compound, watching the cows and looking at the gardens. I got a bright idea to pluck some lemons and put them in my pockets to eat or give to my friends. The lemons belonged to the missionary lady. I was familiar with the garden because I had worked in it many times. I had often thought of these lemons. When we were working, we would eat one or two big tomatoes. Helen had brought seeds from Canada. She loved her garden. Taking and eating from it seemed natural. The cattle were on the garden side so I quickly jumped the stone wall into the orchard. I plucked some lemons and put them in my pocket. I was wearing knickers, which are half pants. I filled my pockets and jumped up onto the other wall.

I sat for a while surveying the area, looking for a good place to land on the other side. I settled my hands on the wall beside me, and when I lifted them, I saw that there was a snake attached. It was a creepy feeling. I cried and tried to shake the snake off. Eventually it fell down among some stones. I cried loud enough that all the hospital patients heard me. I yelled that I was bitten by a snake. Two fellows came with a stick, and they searched for the snake. They never found it.

They immediately took me to the hospital. There was a missionary nurse there. She asked for my hand, and there was blood. She made a small incision with a knife and squeezed out all the blood. I was given something to drink. They put some medicine on the wound and bandaged it. I was told not to sleep, even if I felt sleepy. I should just stay awake.

The technician who cut my finger and made the incision felt my pockets and said, "What's this, lemons?" He asked me where I got them, and soon the whole story came out. I was in trouble for stealing. I tried to explain that perhaps I was not stealing because I always ate when I did some work in the garden. She never mentioned that we should not do that. They looked at me with such a funny look. I asked, "Did I do something wrong?" I did not know what to think anymore. A lady from church came and they related the story to her. She suggested that perhaps the bite was punishment for stealing. That whole day I was not supposed to sleep, but I did fall asleep when they left me in the house. The missionary nurse, Mary Long, came back in during the afternoon. She got very angry, and spanked me. Then I was really wide awake for the rest of the day. I did not die from the snakebite.

Excelling in My Studies

There were many trials of youth, but education, at least at first, was easy for me. I don't know why. I was allowed to skip grades. When I began at school I was seven or eight and the children in my class were six. I read very easily, though, so I jumped two classes, and the next year, another two. When I came to grade five, I found it much more difficult. English was no problem. Somehow I could learn English easily, but with math I struggled. In the sixth class, when they took all the marks, I got the highest in the whole school. The teacher called me to the front, before all the teachers and all the students, and she gave me a presentation. Everybody clapped.

When I was in the sixth class, and my brother was in seventh class. He was eighteen years old and had become a man. He did not study well and had no interest in education. He found a girl in the hostel; together they went to the missionary couple and said they wanted to get married. The couple thought they were too young, but they left together anyway.

Das visits home of second mother, Helen Warkentin.

When my brother left, that was difficult for me. It was during my sixth-year class that Helen returned to Canada. She had been like a mother to me. I began to wonder what would become of me. Though I studied well, someone had to sponsor me. One of the sirs (masters of the school) said that I might not have a future. Because Helen was leaving for a furlough, I might not be able to continue studying. I was very confused at that time.

Sometimes I would skip classes. Another missionary lady came. Her name was Anna Suderman. She was an American and said that she would help me finish my seventh grade.

The Life of Helen Warkentin

Larry Kehler

(The following biographical sketch was compiled from sources in Helen Warkentin's file at the Center for Mennonite Brethren Studies in Winnipeg, Manitoba.)

Helen Leana Warkentin was born on November 25, 1887, in the village of Hoffnungsfeld, near Winkler, Manitoba. Her parents were (Rev.) John and Sarah (Loewen) Warkentin. She had nine siblings (six brothers and three sisters).

On confession of her faith she was baptized and accepted into membership in the Winkler Mennonite Brethren Church on July 17, 1904. She remained a member of this congregation for the rest of her life.

After graduating from the Mennonite Collegiate Institute (MCI) in Gretna, Manitoba, in 1915, getting some teacher training in Manitoba, and doing a year of studies at Moody Bible Institute in Chicago, Helen left for her first term of missionary service in India in December 1919.

Helen was stationed at Deverakonda as a teacher and principal of a boarding school for children, becoming also dietitian, supervisor of gardening, of well digging and carpentry. She took the place of a mother for many orphans and students. Her greatest concern was the spiritual welfare of her pupils.

Prior to her homecoming and retirement from India former students and friends celebrated her 69th birthday in a school reunion. Among other touching tributes to Miss Warkentin, one former student said, "During the tenure of thirty-six years with us, we have grown to love you as our own mother. As the principal, you never assumed an air of superiority. You were too courteous to offend anyone. Many of our orphan children who were dumped into your lap, called you Amma (mother) and you took them. But for your color, you are bone of our bone and pain of our pain. The main traits of your character are your motherly affection, absolute sincerity, and utter humility. Your beloved orphan girls and boys are now some hundreds in number."

Helen Warkentin died in Winkler, Manitoba, on June 25, 1975, at the age of 87.

Larry and Jessie Kehler befriended Das and Doris Maddimadugu in 1976 when they attended Canadian Mennonite Bible College in Winnipeg, Canada. Larry has been a pastor, a former editor of *The Mennonite*, and has served in many capacities with the Mennonite Church in the USA and Canada. Larry is a mission partner with the Maddimadugu's, regularly sharing their news with a network of friends in Canada.

Chapter 2

Youth: Agony of Discouragement and the Gift of Forgiveness

Anna Suderman Becomes My Sponsor

IF I WANTED TO continue school, I would have to go to Mahabub Nagar, another village a hundred kilometers away. Anna was not willing to sponsor me to go to high school at first. Maybe she didn't have the money, but somehow I convinced her and promised that I would study well and do whatever I could to help. So she sent me and another boy named Prakash to high school. We took our boxes on the bus and arrived four hours later.

Anna had put an envelope in my pocket and said that as soon as we got there, we should see the missionary principal and give the letter to him. He would tell us what to do. We were brought into the office, and I stood there as he read the note she had sent. Then he asked "Where is the money?" I was confused and said that I didn't know anything about the money. I checked all my pockets. Prakash also had no money. The warden asked how we expected to be taken into the school without the money. We were taken to the edge of the school grounds, and there we stood all day. We listened to the bell ring for lunch as we stood there, and we were very hungry. We were told we could not come in until we had the money.

In those days there were no telephones. There was no way to call Anna. So we asked if we could have the boxes back that we came with. We stayed outside the whole day, and slept underneath a tree that night. The next day, to our relief they said, "It is here—the money; we found the money." It had been on the table among the papers on the desk where they had opened the envelope. At the time it seemed like a miracle, and it was a great relief to go into the hostel.

Anna Suderman gave me a school uniform, paid for the food, the school fees, hostel fees, and other things like that. That money was sent along with me. But I had no money for books. I had to think of a way to find my books for school. I had a friend who was crippled. He had no legs, but he did have all the books. I made a deal with him. I waited for him to read from all the books before he let me have one, but he was nice. I would carry him to class sometimes. Most of the time, though, I would carry his books and he would crawl. I would read at night, when all would go to sleep at nine o'clock, the hour of curfew. I would sit by the door where there was a little light. Studying like this, I was always tired. But I was good at studies, always in the first five ranks at school.

The Humiliation of Being an Untouchable

One summer when I was home, the high caste people came to call for laborers. I watched them make announcements in the village. I walked along the walls, backwards and forwards, drawing with my finger. I was just playing. Accidentally I had backed into a big man who smacked me full force on the side of the head and knocked me to the ground. It hurt for several days. I realized that not only had I bumped into a man, I had also crossed the caste line in the village. The man was outraged that a Dalit (untouchable) had carelessly touched and defiled him. I never told the elders of our village about this incident because they would have blamed me for not being humble enough. In those days the caste system was deeply accepted by the upper as well as the lower caste people. This was the will of God.

Now that I look back on it, though, I see that he also defiled himself because he voluntarily touched me when he slapped me. That also made him untouchable. But he did not purify himself because he had slapped me. Caste distinctions still play a very large roll in Indian culture, especially in the villages.

Saved from Quicksand by an Angel

In the summer, I stayed with my father who lived alone in his village, in Angadipet, and whatever food he could find is what we would eat. I was carefree. One day I was just walking through the fields. I thought it would be fun to go splash my feet in the water. The puddle was very big, and the farther I went into the puddle the more and more I splashed. As the sun started to set, I began to move out of the puddle. I tried to go backwards and forwards, but I could not budge. I was stuck in quicksand. I looked around and saw that no one was there to help me. As the sun continued to set, it dawned on me that I could not get out. I screamed. It was the only thing I could do. I screamed for so long. But nobody was there.

By then the sun had gone. I saw a lady coming back from the village, or perhaps carrying something from a farm. I called to her for help, shouting "Sayam cheyyandi!" ("Help me!") and "Rakshinchandi!" ("Save me.") She didn't know that I was in the quicksand. I don't know whether she heard me or not. Perhaps she did not want to help. She continued to walk on. I sank a little deeper.

Then I thought I saw another woman coming. I screamed for her to help me too. She also didn't come closer. I was there for some time, and it got much darker. There was no light on the fields. Shadows of birds fell onto the fields.

One more woman came. She appeared from no certain direction. She came into the water a little first and then threw the end of her sari wrap for me to catch hold. I didn't catch it right away. She came in a little further and further still until I could catch hold. She began to pull very slowly. When I came out to my ankles, she took her sari and squeezed the water out. She didn't ask me any questions. She didn't ask me my name or anything. She just walked away. I wanted to follow her. But I couldn't. I was sure she was going through the fields, but it was unusual for a woman to walk through the fields in the dark. I had nothing in my hands, no burden, nothing I was carrying, but still I could not follow her. I lost her in the fields, she was gone. I never asked her who she was. To this day I have not seen her again.

Had she not come, I would have died. I went to see the same place many months later. I was afraid to go near the water, but I was also fascinated by the sight. I heard later that some other children had drowned there.

I wondered about this woman. She could have been twenty or thirty. She was dark-skinned and her sari was red, bright red. I have so many questions about her. I wonder still if she was from my village, and if she was, why I didn't recognize her. I knew all the people in my village, and she was a stranger.

In the villages everyone is divided and known by their caste, and they don't touch you or help you if you are from the untouchable caste. If those first two women were from a higher caste, and if they knew I was from an untouchable caste, perhaps they choose not to come and help me. Perhaps they knew it was quicksand and they simply didn't want to risk it. If this last woman knew who I was and whose son I was, and if she was from my caste, I would have recognized her. All of these questions linger on. When I became a Christian, I could not doubt God's miracles. Maybe what happened was a miracle. I don't know much about angels, but I believe there are more in the world than people think.

Weariness and Despair

But at the time, I did not believe in much at all. I was young, and I became very disillusioned. I was in the ninth class when I began to wonder why I did all this studying and work at school. I had no soap to wash my clothes or oil for my hair. I had a friend named Arthur who was in a similar position. We decided that we would sneak out from the hostel and go work in a mill where they shelled peanuts. They removed the husks and kept the seeds. The workers would fili up sacks all night. We had to carry the sacks from the mill to the warehouse. We both did this till five o'clock, and then they would let us go. Before the school warden would wake up, we would jump over the wall and come back, return, and sleep. We were very tired from doing this nighttime work and from our studies. With the one rupee we earned each night we would buy soap and powder to brush our teeth. I had some other odd jobs and chores at the hostel, but there was no payment for that.

I was tired of studying and working. I thought that I had studied enough already. A few friends like me were also becoming disillusioned. It was in the winter season that we spent much time bunking (skipping) school. This was the season for custard apples. The area around the school is very famous for custard apples, and the apple trees around the school grew wild. We would go to class at about nine o'clock, wait until the attendance was taken, and then excuse ourselves from our different classes. We would meet outside the school on the main road and take off. We would go to the hills and eat the custard apples and roam around. By four o'clock we would come back. The warden would catch us once in a while and beat us, but we were not bothered by that. It was still better than staying in class. We would catch up on our homework and then bunk school again to eat custard apples. When tenth class came, I was ready to quit school.

Running Away

One of my friends said we should run away to a bigger place. I thought this was a good idea, and so I went with three friends, Jayanamdam, Sunder, and Prakash. Jayanamdem said that he would purchase a train ticket. The rest of us would ride without tickets. We wanted to go to the other side of India, so we headed towards Mumbai. We fellows had some money, and we would share everything. We shared one ticket after all. Once in a while the ticket inspectors would come by and ask people for tickets. If you had a ticket, you would show it and they punched it. Then they went away. So Prakash, as soon as the inspector was coming, went into the toilet and closed the door until he left. I kept moving from compartment to compartment, outside the train. I kept moving. I would keep a look-out to see where the inspector was at the time. Sunder lay under a blanket behind some boxes and things. We hid well, but Prakash was found anyway. He thought the ticket inspector went away and so he came out. But the ticket inspector was waiting to catch him.

Prakash told him, "Sir, my mother is very sick sir, and she lives here in Mumbai." The ticket inspector slapped him on the face several times and gave him a good lecture. He was told not to do it again, that Prakash would ruin his life. Then the inspector let him go. We came out, and sat together. We escaped the inspector and soon arrived at the Victoria Traveler Station in Mumbai. There the ticket inspectors wait for the passengers, and each one has to hand over their ticket. We sent Jayanamdam out with his ticket to buy four platform tickets. They are for visitors coming to see off relatives who are leaving by train. He gave one to each of us. We walked out of the gates and could get through without getting caught. We thought that this was much fun.

We went into the city. Jayanamdam had an uncle there, but it was very difficult for us to find him. We roamed the city for days asking people if they knew him, searching everywhere. We found him working in a sweat shop. He was able to find a job for

Jayanamdam, and he found a job for me cleaning a house as a servant.

Sunder and Prakash were still roaming around. We gave them a job. Their job was to go to the ocean and to find out what it was like. We'd never seen this ocean before. Then they would come back and report how it was. It would be as if we got to see it ourselves. We were very curious fellows. In the evening we would have a meal. The people who worked in a shop made chapattis for us, and that was our only meal. Chapattis are a common bread in India, made with Chapatti flour, and fried into a puff. They are fluffy and delicious. Prakash then had got a job at the restaurant, so we would sleep under the tables, and the next morning we would get up and leave before they opened.

After only one week, I said that I felt bad about leaving school. I wanted to go back. The others were angry. "What?! You want to go back? You were the one who said we should leave," they all shouted at me. "I know, but I feel bad. We did not finish school, we did not finish our education. Maybe you think I am a cheat, but nobody back there knew where we were going or that we ran away from the school. Life at the school was much better."

Repentance and Return

They turned their backs on me, and ignored me for days. But soon a couple of them agreed with me; they were feeling the same way. Jayanamdem decided to stay with his relatives. He said there was no way he would return to the school. The rest of us marched back to the station.

Once again, we boarded the train without tickets. We knew that if we were caught, we would be put in prison. Again the inspector came. He showed up when we were halfway to Hyderabad. There was nothing we could do. We sat there and did not hide. When the man came to get the tickets, we told him we had none. He slapped Prakash. Since Prakash looked a little bigger, people assumed he was the leader. We all told the inspector about how we had lied the last time we came like this, and how we ran away from school. We told him we did not like Mumbai, that we wanted to go back, but we had no money or food. We told him that he could do whatever he wanted with us, that this would be OK. He looked at us for a long time, told us to stay seated, and that he would come back.

We sat there in the train compartment—very comfortably. Six hours later, he came back and said that he was going to punish us. He left us sitting there until we arrived in Hyderabad. He came and told us to follow him. We got to the gate and then he walked us out. He told us to never run away again, and to never get on the trains without tickets. He thought that we were honest enough to confess, so we could not be that bad. Because of him, the ticket man did not check us, and we were free again.

That was a very kind act. We were not Christians at the time, and we had no personal belief, even though we were studying at a Christian school. Now that I am a Christian, I see this situation differently.

We went back to school. All the boys and all the girls in the hostel—there were about 500 students—began to boo and shout. The principal was a missionary from Canada, and he was a very big man, a huge man. He approached and said, "I will take you and I will punish you." He took us behind the store room, and he took off his belt, but he didn't hit us too much. For one week we were punished every day. He told us that we would have to work for a week with no food, and asked us if we would agree. We did, so we would go out and pull the weeds and that was our punishment. We received no food, just as he said.

Prakash was very clever, and he figured out a way for us to get some food. He made an exchange with the cooks. We would do some cooking for them, and also fetch the firewood. Everyone would come with their plates, but before they were served we would eat some half-cooked rice. Then we would wash the plates. The principal would say, "This is good punishment for you." He didn't know that we were eating food.

After the week he asked us if we were "sensible" and asked if we would do it again. He said we would have to wait for the missionary who sent us here. We would have to confess and ask forgiveness of her because she was paying for us. Anna Suderman came. Sunder's parents paid his fees, but Anna was paying for Prakash and me.

A Load Off My Heart

Anna called me in first. I stood in front of her and told her what I had done. She asked me all the details, what we ate, how long the trip was, how we got there with no tickets. Finally she said, "The real question is this: Who instigated this? Whose idea was it?" I said, "Prakash." He was so big for his age, it was easy to believe. Even now, he is a big man. He is a hunter now, and is well known. He stayed on in the village and now lives in Helen Warkentin's old house. He is a good man.

After I told Anna that it was Prakash who had the idea to run away, she asked me if I would seek forgiveness. I told her I did, and I knelt down in front of her. She put her hand on me and told me that for whatever I said that was true, I was forgiven.

When I went out, I saw Prakash there with his mother. He asked me what I told her and I said that I revealed nothing. I listened by the door when he went in, and I heard Anna ask him if he was the one that instigated the run away. He denied it, saying, "No, no, it was this other fellow." She said that it must be him, because Das would never tell lies. She told him that she was going to cut off the help that she was giving him. She was not happy. When he came out of the room, he chased me around the trees.

Even after we returned, I felt restless. Around this time, an evangelist came to town preaching, and every night he was calling for repenters to come forward. On the last day, I felt something stirring in me. I felt that I had done wrong to Prakash and had not told the whole truth to the missionary lady. I walked into the church, and I knocked on the door of the pastor. I told him that God was speaking to me. He asked me to kneel down to tell him everything that I had done, and to pray to God. So I told him about the Mumbai train, and I told him about lying about Prakash. And he said that tomorrow I would come to see him at ten o'clock.

When I woke the next morning I felt different, I felt light-hearted. I felt peace. I went to him at 10 o'clock and told him how I was feeling, and I asked him what was wrong. He said that there was nothing wrong, but that I had a load on my heart, but now it was gone. I felt saved. So that is how I began to experience prayer. He instructed me to get baptized, and I took some classes. Before baptism I had to confess to lots of people, not just Prakash. I went to Anna Suderman, and I confessed to her that I had told lies about Prakash. She had known that something was wrong. But she had trusted me. She told me that I must ask forgiveness from Prakash. After I considered it, I decided that I had to ask for forgiveness from everyone I had hurt. And then I was baptized. That was my conversion experience.

·

Chapter 3

Young Adulthood: Survival, Ambition, and Service

One Year of Bible School

I WANTED TO CONTINUE school. I took one year of Bible school. I learned about Scripture, Christian values, and the church, but I was also able to learn deeper things about my faith. I was thinking about the next steps to take in my life, and how to survive. I wondered who would give me a job, and how could I find reimbursement for my services. The Bible school did not prepare me for that. I completed my training, and then I returned to Devarakonda and talked to the principal. I asked him if I could find a job in the school. Even though I only studied high school and Bible school and had no previous training for a teaching position, he told me to come back after one week, and then he had a job for me. I was offered a position as a Telugu teacher for the lower classes. Because I was not qualified for teaching, I was given only fifty rupees per month. That was very little for one person to survive on. I took it even though the sweeping attendant earned ninety rupees a month. The principal also gave me a room in the hostel, separate from the boys. As a teacher, he said, I should have my own room.

I cooked my own food and paid for personal necessities. It was absolutely not enough. And I did not exactly look the part.

I looked like one of the students, with no proper clothes. One day my friend Robert saw me wearing a tattered shirt, and he was upset. He told me that teachers were supposed to have nicer clothes. He wanted to give me a shirt. So he brought me home and handed me this blue shirt. He was much taller and bigger than me. His mother was kind, took the shirt, and fitted it to me. Now I had the one shirt, and at night I would wash it and dry it and press it under some books. I had a shirt, but food was still a problem. I could not get enough rice to cook. But I ate what I could buy or find, and I survived.

During this time I also taught Sunday school. I knew Bible stories and verses. As a child I learned many verses by memory, what you might say are the golden verses. During school I would teach Telugu and teach Hindu stories about mythical creations and animals speaking. On Sunday I would teach from the Bible.

Lab Tech Training

I finished one year there and began to wonder where I would go next. At the time there was a young missionary named Peter Block, a doctor from Saskatchewan in Canada. I talked to him about what I could do, and he said that there was one woman who had started to offer laboratory technician training. I asked how I could do this. I now had one year of teaching experience. This would be a totally different thing, but I thought that I could do it. She said that I would have to pay for the schooling, but that I could borrow some money from a fund that the missionaries had started. I would have to pay it back.

I went in for an interview. Quite a few young men came for the interview. Some were not well prepared, I could tell. When they interviewed me they asked if I would commit myself to go to any hospital they sent me to. I said I would, and I answered their questions to the best of my ability. When the interview was finished, they told me I got the job.

I was sent to study for six months at one of the more well-known medical institutions in Hyderabad, and then I came back to the Mennonite missions and I worked there for one year. There were two lab technicians who were senior to me. They always gave me the lower type of work. I mixed blood and spun test tubes. They never let me use the microscope or do the findings. Soon I became very good at my work. Whenever they were not doing things, I would look under the microscope at the germs and bacteria. I would see them move around, and I would become very excited. I liked my job.

Other Odd Jobs and an Honesty Test

Somehow a doctor by the name of Friesen came to like me and gave me odd jobs to do. One day the doctor's wife came to see me, took me by the hand, and said she had an exciting job for me. She asked me if I knew how to ride a bicycle. She gave me a bag and told me to take it to the post office. I would do that every day. I collected the mail from the post office, and put it in a container, and they locked it. So I began to go and bring her mail, and sometimes boxes. First I was Das the lab technician, and then I was Das the postal boy. I did that for nine months or so and I liked it; I could race the cars.

After these nine months, Mrs. Friesen came again. She told me that I was doing well and that she wanted to give me another job. She asked me to go to the medical store and return with medicines for the hospital. There was more money involved with this work. She told me that next year, if I worked there, they would increase my salary by five rupees. Those were mission salaries. In the evenings I would go to my room in the Mennonite office building. I would wash my face and think of my friends who were drinking tea. I had no tea.

Even though it was not much money at that time, I still managed to make my loan payments, and I survived. One day Mrs. Friesen gave me my salary in an envelope. I counted it out, and there were the five extra rupees for my raise, but there were still eighty extra rupees besides. I took the extra money back to her and told her that she had overpaid me. She apologized and said she forgot.

Perhaps she was testing me, because, for three months this continued to happen. There would be extra money. One evening Mrs. Friesen came to my room. She brought some buns for me, and told me to eat. She asked me if I realized that she had given extra money. When I told her I did know, she expressed gratitude for my honesty. I told her that I didn't want to keep the money because it was not mine. She began to take a liking to me.

She even asked me to come to her house. When I went there, there was another family, a husband and wife who were buffalo keepers and farmers, and they had a small son named Johnny. They were good people, and it was nice to be around a family. Johnny and I became friends. I would take his tricycle and push it around and we played volleyball as well.

Dr. Friesen called me up one day and asked me to take a different place where a lab technician had left. I went there and worked. At that time the Mennonite Christian Fellowship Service of India was thinking of sending someone from India out into the missionary field to preach. They were also looking to take medical people, doctors and nurses. I asked if they would take lab technicians. One of the mission men, a very nice man said, "Why not?" They hadn't talked about it, but they decided that they would let me go if it could be worked out. There were Swiss, Americans, Germans, and Filipinos going out to Vietnam.

I Meet Doris

I packed and went to Kolkata, to the central office. They gave me a room in the Mennonite Central Committee (MCC) building until my transit for Vietnam was arranged. I had to wait for my visa, because it was not processed, and it took about nine months for it to arrive. During these nine months I visited a Mennonite church, where I met my then-future wife, Doris.

At that time, her mother was looking for a husband for her. There were a few Christian young men around, but she wanted someone who was from the south of India. She did not want anyone from Kolkata because the food and culture were different than that of the south. Her brother-in-law knew her mother was looking for someone, and he brought me home to her house, and I talked with them for a while. I told Doris that I was going away to Vietnam, which was at war and that I could not marry her right then because I didn't know what would happen to me. I told her mother that Doris could wait if she wished. If nothing happened to me while I was in Vietnam, then when I returned, we could marry. During the time I was waiting, I was sent to the Bangladesh border to distribute food, blankets, clothing, and all kinds of things for refugees. Doris was working for the Mennonite Central Committee's office in Kolkata, and we wrote letters to each other while I was gone.

Reflecting on Survival, Ambition, and Service

I think that all my life experiences were a process, making me the person that I am today. Through the initial stages, my main concern was survival. But when I took these steps in order to survive, *I found an ambition within myself* to become somebody and to achieve something. I went to the missionary compound to survive, and in many ways, to high school for the same reason. But in doing so, I learned that I wanted to educate myself as much as possible. I began to attend lots of meetings on my own, to seek my purpose in *life*. I wanted something much more substantial in my life. At this time I had no great ambition to serve, or to be useful. I just wanted to be somebody. Vietnam, as it happened, was an opportunity. I discovered that if I would raise my hand, I would have a chance to do something. I was young, and those were the thoughts on my mind.

But even then, when I was just trying to survive and make a name for myself, Helen Warkentin played an important role in my life. Whatever I did, I always remembered her and how she did things for others. Her face would always surface. So, when I volunteered for things, it is true, I did it to survive. But I thought that maybe I would also get the opportunity to study one day and to help somebody. I wanted to survive, but the path I took was not an easy one. Volunteers going to Vietnam only earned thirty rupees a month, plus room and board. I think that Helen influenced me, and she is partly responsible for giving me the will to take the harder path.

Taking Relief Supplies to Eastern Pakistan

Bangladesh was still Eastern Pakistan at the time. There was much political turmoil because the power was concentrated in the West. We would take a large truck of clothes, and I would distribute them to refugees who were shivering and cold. We would also feed them. I did this work because I remembered how I had sought a means of survival for myself. I changed and my perspective changed. It was a continuous process. I always thought of Helen Warkentine. But now Doris and her family also influenced me, and the people from church would gather around me.

Doris Tells Her Story

Doris Maddimadugu,
as told to Julia Guyer and Andrea Buchanan

We grew up in a Christian family and were very much doted-on by our parents. We attended church and always said family prayers and had daily devotions together. My father played the violin, and we did a lot of singing.

Whenever we sang off tune, our father corrected us. That's how we got good at singing, because we sang and sang and really enjoyed it.

We lived in Kolkata and my father was an elder for the Tamil and Telugu church where we attended. But since we spoke English at home and did not really understand Telegu or Tamil, we children attended a Baptist Sunday school. It was only after my father's retirement that we moved to Orissa. It was very close to the beach where we bought a house, a small two-room house where the four of us lived, my younger sister and I, dad and mum. My oldest brother and sister were away from home, in an English-medium boarding school.

To be honest, my father really loved us girls. It's not that my mother didn't. But if you spend a lot of time in India, you'll see that the mothers often care more for their sons, and the fathers will care for their daughters. My job at home was to dust, sweep, and tidy everything. Father always had lots of stones in the windows. While I would tidy and settle everything, Father would say "No, no keep these things in their place." And I would laugh and say, "No, I'm not moving them, I am just removing the dust and putting things back." So it was much fun during that time when the four of us lived together. Then Father passed away.

After my father died, my older brothers and sisters moved to Kolkata to live with my aunt and finish school there. My mother was going to put my younger sister and me in a boarding school. But I did not like this plan because I wanted to be with the rest of our family. So, we went to Kolkata and waited eight months until our admission was accepted in an English school.

We found a church that felt comfortable; it was very small but we were like one family. It was called Emmanuel Chapel founded by the United Missionary Society, and we attended there. Even growing up in a Christian family I never had a personal experience of spirituality and at Emmanuel Chapel I experienced the ministry of John Hamilton. During that time I committed myself, accepted Jesus, and was baptized in water. I also gave my testimony in the church. If my father had been alive he would have been very happy to see me, but he was gone by then.

After I finished school, I took some further training in shorthand, as a typist, and in bookkeeping. My younger sister continued her studies, but I needed to work to support the family because my second sister and I were the only earning members. My mother got a pension and my brother took a position playing violin. I thank God for keeping us together as a family.

Eventually I got a job with the Mennonite Central Committee in Kolkata working in their central office. During this time I first met Das.

Das and Doris at the Mennonite World Conference in Kolkata, 1997

Serving with MCC in War-Torn Vietnam

I was excited to go to Vietnam. The nine months of waiting were long for me. On February 26th, 1968, I went to Vietnam. In two years, I saw a world of change. I moved from Devarakonda to smaller towns where I taught school, to bigger cities like Kolkata, and then immediately into the middle of a country at war. It was the time of the Tet Offensive, the Vietcong had invaded South Vietnam and killed many, many American soldiers and Vietnamese civilians. I landed only a couple weeks after the invasion. The experience was horrifying. I had friends in the Vietnam Christian Service in Saigon. They came from all denominational backgrounds—Lutherans, Baptists, Pentecostals, Mennonites. There were many internationals also from Europe and Asian Countries. It was a strange and different life.

I took Vietnamese language study for three months before going to the Nhatrang, the village where I worked for two years. I liked the culture and learned to eat noodles. I made many Western friends. I got a glimpse into Western life through these people. I learned how different I was from them. Many of them came there at their own expense; they knew that they had jobs waiting for them when they returned. They were not worried about surviving. It was strange to me. Never before had I reached out my hand like this to others.

The War Child

Phong was nine years old
And lived on the beach in summer and in the cold.
She played in the sand at the Honchon caves,
Sang melodies to the rumbling waves;
She waved at the moon and whistled to the wind,
And talked in whispers to the hills beyond.
Phong was the offspring of a cruel war

Which left on her mind a lasting scar.
Who cares to know the sorrow and pain
Of a beautiful child who's gone insane?

—Das Maddimadugu: Vietnam 1968

Our Friendship Goes Back Forty Years

Jeannie Stuckey, as told to David Janzen: October 2010

Our friendship with Das goes back more than forty years. We first met him while we were in Vietnam with the Mennonite Central Committee. Allen, my husband, had finished his residency as a physician and, right after that, in September 1969, we went to Vietnam with our two-month-old son Jonathan. After language study we were in Nha Trang near the ocean, where Allen was busy with medical work. Das worked as a lab technician. We would meet whenever all the MCC service workers came together. It was an international group with Americans, Swiss, Philippinos, and Das from India. He stood out from the group because of his very dark skin and infectious joi de vivre. He loved to take the Honda scooter into town after hours to make Vietnamese friends in a way that we could not. This was when Das was still a single man. A few years later, Das and his wife Doris, with baby Esther, had another term with MCC in Vietnam that ended in 1975, with their evacuation in a plane-load of orphans.

Das's adventuresome character stands out for me in that he took his turn escorting the MCC women to their house at night because he knew what to do if they encountered cobras. We were often threatened by thieves trying to hotwire and steal our vehicles. One night Das slept on the carport roof in case something would happen. When a thief drove away with our Landrover, Das and Loel Jantzi ran after them on foot, taking a short-cut to the oceanside road, and managed somehow to get the car back. That took a lot of energy and courage, which we all celebrated the next morning when they told the story.

Jeannie Stuckey and her husband, Dr. Allen Stuckey, live in Elkhart IN. They served with the Mennonite Central Committee in Vietnam from 1969 to 1972. Jeannie finds joy in sponsoring a Bindu Home child.

Marriage with Doris

I returned to India in May or June of 1970. Doris had been living in the United States, working in the Trainee Exchange Program through the Mennonite church. She returned in August, and by October her mother had settled our engagement. Things were different then. We were not allowed to go out together. Only after we were officially engaged could we go out, and even then, we had to be back by seven in the evening.

Weddings are the most important occasion and celebration in Indian culture. We wanted to be practical while still observing some traditions. I was staying with a Canadian family in the area. My father had died by this point. I only had my brother and his family, and they could not come to the wedding. I went to my wedding alone, but it was a good event. A normal Indian wedding has between 1000 and 1500 people. We had about 500. The wedding was very western, with the traditional maid of honor and best man.

Another Term in Vietnam and a Desperate Flight

After the wedding, we lived some time in Kolkata. I had a job at a hospital and Doris worked in the Mennonite Central Committee's office. We had our first child, Esther. Life was busy. But I felt a call to try and do something more. We decided as a family to return to Vietnam. Doris was given the job of taking care of all the staff's rooms and meals. I was doing medical work. For some time we lived on the beach, but we were soon sent in closer to the mountains to work among the tribal people. We had only six months left of our two-year term when suddenly we were told that all the MCC staff had to come to a meeting in Saigon. The first day we were there, the Vietcong came shooting and burning houses. We decided to stay inside on the second day. On that very same day, as soon as the meeting was over, our people began to leave the country. It was great chaos. The Americans were all getting out. We had nowhere to go, though. One of the first flights leaving was a plane carrying babies to America. There were two of these planes. But we were not allowed to board a plane. We were told that only one of us could go, either Doris or I, but not Esther. We prayed and decided that we would all go, or none of us would go.

We were feeling desperate. Then a missionary couple who had worked with us said they would talk to the people in charge of boarding. They thought perhaps there might be a need for more people to look after the babies on the flight. The babies were children of American soldiers who had been born to Vietnamese mothers who could not provide for them. We learned later that these children were put up for adoption in the U.S. Finally, we were told that we could fly on the plane if we helped with these children. There were sixty children. They were so tiny and innocent, and we gave them food and milk. We watched out the window as the first plane with babies took off. They were not yet five miles away when their plane crash landed from mechanical failure. Doris did not see it. We were terrified, but the pilots decided to take off anyway. It was a long flight.

South China Sea—An Unknown Cause

The sea raged outrageously
Standing on her head,
She swayed and raved
In a mad fury.

> She hissed, and pushed me back.
> Held me prisoner.
> For longer than I could endure.
> When I tried to free myself
> A crest-fallen wave tugged at my sleeve,
> And implored me to not leave.
> Then I knew that all the rumbling
> Was not rage.
> The spray from the waves were
> The halting tears of a grieving mother
> Who sacrificed her children
> In a war to an unknown cause.

—Das Maddimadugu: Vietnam 1969

With MCC in Kansas and College at CMBC

The plane dropped children off at locations all over the country. Finally we arrived in New York. But then we had nowhere to go. We had nowhere to stay. We did not even have proper visas. The missionary couple who had helped us get onto a flight, Luke and Dorothy Beidler, told us that we could stay with their parents. MCC was looking for us. When they found us in Pennsylvania, we were transferred to Newton, Kansas. I helped with the administration of the MCC Relief Center there and Doris helped the women fold clothing for distribution when it came in. During the six months in Newton, we made friends with David and Joanne Janzen and others at New Creation Fellowship.

I began to correspond with the Canadian Mennonite Bible College and was accepted. So when our six months with MCC were over, we went to Winnipeg to study, and there our daughter Jessica was born.

For a time we lived as "parents" in a halfway house in Winnipeg. I remember, Bob, a French Canadian boy with a juvenile criminal record. We kind of liked him and wanted to help him out. Several times he gave us headaches by going out in the night, hotwiring cars, but eventually he evened out. At the end of our term with the half way home, we felt very close to the boys, and it was difficult to move away. But we kept contact with them, even when we returned to the CMBC dorm. There Bob visited us several times, and others also came. Because of the nature of the living conditions at CMBC, we could not entertain the young men as much as we would have liked.

At times it felt like I did not have the capacity to complete the study program because of the language problems and because of the heaviness of the courses, but I pulled through. In 1978, I graduated from CMBC, majoring in theology. Having two children, Doris really managed well, looking after the family plus taking care of my personal needs.

I studied at CMBC for three years and at the Overseas Mission Study Center in New Jersey for one year. All the time we were preparing with the thought that we must go back to India. For us India means Andhra Pradesh, where I grew up, an area where there is more need than in many other situations.

Traveling Light

Mary and Luke Martin

We have had the privilege of meeting Devadass (Das) Maddimadugu in three countries. In July 1967 we visited India for a few days when we were returning to the United States with our two young children after five years in Vietnam. It was Das, working in Kolkata while waiting for a visa to enter Vietnam, who showed us a place at the MCC office to sleep for the night.

We next met Das in Vietnam when he served as a laboratory technician with Mennonite Central Committee at the Evangelical clinic and hospital in Nha Trang in 1968 and 1969. Since we lived and worked with the Mennonite Mission in Saigon, we had little association with the MCC team in Nha Trang. Das and Yoshihiro Ichikawa from Japan were the two Asian Mennonites who made significant contributions among the Mennonite Central Committee volunteers to Vietnam Christian Service whose personnel were overwhelmingly North American.

It was when Das returned to Vietnam in 1973 with Doris and baby Esther that our friendship developed. Das was then the laboratory technician at the Evangelical clinic and hospital in Pleiku. On our visits to Pleiku and their visits to Saigon we learned to appreciate their gentle spirit and the simplicity of their way of life. We enjoyed wonderful Indian dishes that Doris cooked up and still use her recipes for real Indian curry and coconut rice.

We returned to Pennsylvania in 1976. When Das and Doris were studying at the Overseas Missionary Study Center at Ventnor, New Jersey, we and our three children went to visit them. Sometime later they visited us at our home in Allentown PA. The weekend luggage for their family of four consisted of a flat attaché case and a bag of diapers for Jessica. I (Mary) was inspired to set goals for traveling lighter, but I have never been able to match that!

Luke and Mary Martin were missionaries in Vietnam with Eastern Mennonite Missions where they met Das Maddimadugu in 1973. Luke worked for many years as a caseworker for Vietnamese clients at a social service center in Souderton, PA and has returned several times to Vietnam with tour groups.

Precious Times in India, Canada, and the USA

Annie Janzen: September 2010

When Das and Doris and their daughter Esther lived in the student residence at Canadian Mennonite Bible College in Winnipeg in the 1970s, I was the head cook there. When I had a free Sunday, they would invite me to join them and other students for very tasty chicken curry and rice meals. Their daughter Jessica was born while they were at CMBC, and I recall a picnic where I was privileged to hold the new black-haired baby.

After Das graduated from CMBC, they moved to New Jersey, to the Overseas Ministry Study Center. I travelled there by train to visit them. When Das and Doris and their family returned to Hyderabad, I began gathering funds to support them in their work.

Later I had the opportunity to visit them in Hyderabad. From there Das and I took a bus ride to his home village of Angadipet. Arriving at the crossroads, we could not find a rickshaw, so we began walking. While on the way someone on a bicycle passed us and heralded our coming to others in the village. When we arrived many people had gathered at Das's brother's inner courtyard.

As a guest I was invited to move farther in to sit on a chair. While Das introduced me, I became aware of a young child being held by its mother. The child threw up green vomit. The mother passed the child on to someone else and quickly went to pick up some moist dung from the area where their cow stood at night. She skillfully wrapped the dung around the vomit and placed it on the compost pile. One of the few chickens around had been caught and cooked. The sun had set, and a very tiny Cole oil lamp hung in the courtyard while we ate our supper of curried chicken, rice, and vegetables.

Then we walked to the church, where the people had gathered. The young men improvised a wire to hang a single light bulb for an evening meeting. Two chairs had been placed on the platform area of the church. This is where Das and I were invited to sit. I was honoured with a garland hung around my neck. I was asked to make a speech and became aware that as Das was interpreting, he used more words than I had used. I thought "He is making what I said sound better to the ears of the listeners." The scripture reading was accompanied by drum music. Young girls sang several songs.

After the service, two beds were brought into the meeting place. One was placed on the platform for me, and the other was placed in the middle of the building for Das. A Cole oil lamp near Das's bed burned low all night. People brought in mats and slept near the entryway, which didn't have a door yet. A light breeze blew during the full-moon night. There was total silence. I wore a sari, for which I was grateful, since there was no mattress, blanket or pillow on the bed. After a refreshing sleep, we walked to Das's brother's home, where we were each given a six-inch twig from a Neem tree with which we could clean our teeth. The sap inside the twig cleans, whitens and strengthens the teeth. I had earlier observed how white and strong all the people's teeth looked. I kept the twig. It is now in a row of jars of various sizes on my shelf which I use to my life's story.

The bicycle transport took us back to the crossroads teahouse for breakfast, where we awaited the bus. The young daughters of the teahouse owner were cleaning the dishes—all of stainless steel—by scrubbing them with wood ash and then rinsing them in a pail of water. A crowded bus arrived. We managed to squeeze in and return to Hyderabad.

During a later visit to India, Das and I again travelled to Angedipet. This time the electricity was in full use, resulting in much noise from radios. A stone wall was under construction around Das's brother's property in the village. A well provided water for rice, sweet limes, and other crops grown on the farmland Das and Doris own.

Esther, Das, and Doris's eldest, returned to Canada and studied at Canadian Mennonite Bible College, graduating in 1995. Then she went on to study at the Associated Mennonite Biblical Seminary in Elkhart, Indiana, where she met Brent Graber, whom she married.

During the 1990 Mennonite World Conference in Winnipeg, I hosted Das and Doris. When Doris came to the US and Canada in 1998 to visit their daughters, Esther and Jessica, I hosted her while she was in Winnipeg. We went to see my garden during that time.

On June 8, 2009, when Das and Doris visited Canada and the US, I was privileged to host them again for a brunch in my apartment along with Jake and Helen Wiebe who were students with Das years ago in CMBC.

Over the years I've sent Das and Doris cards for their birthdays and anniversaries—which always calls for a little more effort to get the stamp right.

Annie Janzen was head cook at the Canadian Mennonite Bible College in Winnipeg, Canada, for many years and there met Das and Doris in the late 1970's. She has traveled the world visiting her friends and now lives at the Bethel Place residence for retired persons. She enjoys gardening, cooking, and membership in the Grain of Wheat Congregation.

Chapter 4

Our Calling among the People
Where I Was Raised

A Decade in Hyderabad

WE HAD THE OPPORTUNITY to become landed immigrants both in the United States and Canada. Doris and I prayed about that. We would have liked to stay, but God told us to go back home, and we did.

We spend a little time in Kolkata after returning to India, then we went to Hyderabad. I approached the Menonnite Brethern Conference and offered myself to work in any capacity they might offer, but they were reluctant to accept me. They said they had not sent me for higher studies, therefore they had no vacancy for me. Only those who are sent by the mission were taken back and provided with jobs because the mission felt an obligation to utilize their services. So I asked again, several places, until I found a teaching job at an evening Bible college in the city of Hyderabad. Then also the Shemshabad Bible College offered me a position, if I could provide my own local travel, coming and going thirty kilometers. I didn't have that kind of money, but I said "OK, I'll do it" and I continued for two years teaching at Shemshabad.

Later on the Mennonite Brethren Conference asked me to start an English-speaking congregation because by then the international community was moving in. There had been an increase in international visitors, from USA, Canada, and Japan. Doris and I began to relate to people, and invited them to join us. In 1982, we started this MB English church service in the city of Hyderabad. In three years the congregation grew quite big, about two or three hundred people. It was mostly a moving population, ex-patriots, students from seminary and bible colleges. We were able to baptize around eight young men and women the first time and other groups each year. So we kept on adding numbers and we felt very good about it.

A Christian friend, John Reynolds, sold us his small house as he was moving to the States. We managed on my two small salaries, and were able to get our children into a good school. So I taught at a college while I pastored the church. Doris would teach Sunday school and work with the women. It was a very busy time for us. During these years our son Nathan was born.

As a Mennonite Brethren Pastor in Hyderabad

Reverend P. Menno Joel: October 2010

I am privileged to have a long-time friendship with Brother M. B. Devadass (Das) and Mrs. Doris Devadass, co-workers in the Lord in the context of the Mennonite Brethren Church of India.

As a pastor in Hyderabad, Brother Devadass was dynamic and active. He trained a team of leaders and practiced collegiality in the ministry, which enabled many young people to use their talents meaningfully for the glory of God and for the edification of the church. Under his leadership the churh was lively, vibrant, and active with many activities for fellowship and strengthening of the brotherhood.

He was an able administrator and a good leader in his role as the secretary of the Governing Council of the Mennonite Brethren Church. As the Executive Director of the Board of Evangelism, he initiated many programs and brought various wings of ministry under one umbrella to have more efficient management and avoid duplication of the work.

Sister Doris is an able companion to Brother Devadass. She is a quiet but dynamic person, active in women's ministry and Christian education. She gave leadership in the women's wing of the church. Her concern and interest was to uplift the poor and rural women and teach them various income generating skills for their livelihood.

Brother Devadass has had much international exposure and many opportunities to live a sophisticated life, but he chose to live in a remote and insignificant village of India as the center of his work with minimum facilities, and many are blessed through his ministry.

As this family continues to serve the Lord in this part of our country and continues to be a blessing to many, may the Lord be their portion and guide in the days to come.

Rev. P. Menno Joel is pastor of the Bethlehem Mennonite Brethren Church in Malakpet, Hyderabad. He is the former principal of the M. B. Bible Institute, academic dean of the M. B. Bible College in Shamshabad, and treasurer of the M.B. Church of India.

Village Evangelism Development Association

But I felt a growing interest to return to my roots in Andhra Pradesh, to work among the poor and downtrodden people. They are the kind of people that I grew up with. But the Conference said firmly, "No." Then I said, "I'm sorry but I have to move on."

So Doris and I started a rural ministry called VEDA, which means Village Evangelism Development Association. And the problems started with the government officials asking us, "Why don't you register with the government?" So I applied. Then the officials said there was no way I could get a foreign contribution act number, because VEDA is an acronym which contains "evangelism." They told me to remove that word and it would be OK. But I didn't feel like doing it for eight years, and I could not receive any foreign donations. Finally I relented. We changed the whole thing and made the organization's name "Matilda Education Society."

So we began church planting, Sunday schools, summer vacation schools, and health clinics in the villages that we came into contact with. There was a lot of interest among the young pastors we met. We were discovering a new theory, a new way of sharing the word. We began to accept and work with these new pastors, believing that the Lord would provide for us as he had through the previous obstacles in our ministry.

I Am That I Am

I am he that I am.
Don't misunderstand who I am.
I am not the great I AM.
Nor am I an insignificant worm,
But I am also not the same
Who you think that I am.
But I am the one when called
Who will answer, "Lo, here I am."

—Das Maddimadugu

Informal Schools among Tribal People

Though we lived in the city of Hyderabad, we often returned to the area where I was raised and where I received my education. We had no big plans. I would spend time around the villages; I would see the children and their living conditions.

We would collect these children from each village. There might be twenty or twenty-five of them. We would employ girls from the same village who had a little education. Usually these girls had only completed 8th or maybe 10th class. They would look after these children. We had no good school buildings at the time. We held school under a metal roof or a little porch. Sometimes we would use cattle sheds. We began informal schools like this, mostly in tribal hamlets.

Visit to a Tribal Night School

Julia Guyer: Journal

December 2009: Much of the work by Das and Doris has been with the tribal people in the surrounding rural areas. The majority of the children taken into the Bindu Home are from tribal backgrounds, some with perhaps one parent still alive, many with a tribal grandparent, all struggling to support these lowly students, the single hope for their entire families.

During an interview, Das explained that their nonprofit organization funds several institutions, the two larger schools being the main output with various other offshoots. An example of this is the more rudimentary night schools in the tribal hamlets for young people interested in learning, who spend all their daylight hours at work. These young people aren't some American idea of disgruntled high school dropouts; they are often quite young children who come from the underbelly of poverty, families too poor to support these new mouths to feed. They work because there is no option, often indentured for their labor to cover the mere expense of their own existence. And even after a day filled with back-breaking labor, these children are hungry for any kind of learning and volunteer their evenings to the most basic forms of schooling. These offshoot education facilities are termed, simply, "The Night School".

As Das was telling about it, he offered to someday take me along to see one for myself. Of course I jumped at the chance. We drove out to a tribal hamlet about ten kilometers away from where we lived. It was dark, no streetlamps, so I had no sense of bearing other than what the headlights of the car pushed into the darkness. We turned off the main paved road and, without changing pace, drove down a bumpy dirt path for about a kilometer more. Then we came upon a grouping of short windowless houses, shacks, and tents set up within a low cement and rock wall. We parked the car in the middle of a path cut through the center of these structures.

A crowd of people had gathered, anticipating our arrival. I wondered if they were attracted by the lights of the car, or perhaps they knew ahead of time that this car carried one young, white, single, American female—me. Deep breath. Get out of the car.

The building, more like an un-building to me, had a low fabric awning and a dim light coming from inside. It had four walls made of piled and somewhat grouted rock, but no roof. The floor was dirt and gravel, or maybe just little bits of rock that crumbled off the walls. This was way beyond the realm of the English-speaking world. Here, most of the tribal people don't even speak Telugu, the state language. Their mother tongue is believed to be ancient, older than any states or kingdoms in these parts. They are proud to speak it and to teach it to their children. At Das's insistence, or perhaps simply out of profound respect for him, most of the night schools are in Telugu, though often translating from their common tribal tongue.

The linguistic aspect here is central, because their education methods are nearly all oral. When Das told us the instruction was basic, he was being generous. It is primitive at best, primeval even. Although learning through the passing on of oral histories is an ancient and atavistic tradition, seeing it in person seemed to scream of nothing but the wide-open gaping lack of any other resources or possibilities.

Imagine a crumbling roofless shack with a paltry gathering of children inside, sitting obediently on a pile of rocks and gravel, their little brown bodies half bare in the chilly winter night. OK, so maybe I am getting a little dramatic, but walking into that room was one of the most real and dramatic things I have ever been a witness to. The limit of human life in that "room" cannot be adequately compared to the supposed limits of existence that I've experienced. It feels mean because it is. "Why lies he in such mean estate" refers to something real to me now, malnourishment sure, but the elephant in the room was the exposed absence in their completely having nothing. It's beyond any conception we could have of "simple". It is being stripped bare, or more so, just bare in the first place. Naked. Literally. Half of these kids don't even have pants, let alone things to write with or books to read from. They try to learn the alphabet and to write by drawing in the dirt with a stick. That's it . . . all the materials they have for a school: four walls opening to the sky, one jutting electric bulb to ward off the dampening dark, and a stick.

But these kids, about thirty of them ranging in age from three to sixteen, appear hopeful because these people found them and want to teach them the alphabet in Telugu with that dumb little stick. They smile real big, they dance amid much giggling, they stand up on the rock pile and sing. The teachers do all this nearly for free, a paltry thirty rupees a month paid by the Matilda Education Society. Sometimes they walk around with the students pointing to things, saying the name first in the tribal tongue and then in Telugu, hoping that if these kids can speak the state language perhaps it will improve their lot in life by some margin. Maybe they will become more valuable to someone else, shifting from burden to asset. The teachers work here because they feel themselves to be teachers in the old sense, I dare say in the Christian sense. They teach because someone first taught them. "I love therefore I teach."

The poverty in the tribal hamlets is easy to consider typical of the underdeveloped world. Contemporary society has typified this image by generalizing it, removing its particularity, mass producing it and dumping seemingly endless resources into it. And we've barely scratched the surface, let alone altered the course of its reality. Charity organizations take pictures of these kids and make pamphlets out of them and mail them to every home in America. Missionaries (ahem) travel half-way around the world to bring supplies and medicine and help, to do good. Half the time I think we can only be making things worse, going in there with our sun lotion, cameras, and money belts. Those suffering in squalor no longer have faces. Rather, the universal face of poverty looms over us in our abundance, pointing Uncle Sam's finger, and striking responses contrived from guilt.

But the beauty of the night school is that it is deeply rooted in its own people and culture. It acts silently, hands unseen by the deep pockets that typify and neglect, or worse, maybe even compete with the work they are doing. In the tribal culture, a non-tribal person is often viewed as an outsider. Even Das, who grew up as an untouchable, and is a fellow Indian, feels honored that they accept him among them.

He himself once came to the schools to teach, drawing in the dirt with a stick, driven by the need to share the education he was given with his neighbors. It is the organically derived community of shared lack in also sharing your blessings, not just counting them. Yet, when he describes what he was doing then, beginning what would become the night schools, he says he just went to the hamlets to "hang out". To celebrate in their culture or sit around and talk, getting to know each other and building relationships. It was odd of him, even then, to come here. Your average villager does not come to these hamlets to "hang out." There seems to be an agreed-upon division between the tribal people and the rest of Indian culture.

The women wear traditional garb, full flowing skirts, a long headdress which billows out behind them as they walk, and chest coverings with intricately designed bits of mirror and embroidery flashing proudly in the sun. To top this distinction, they also like to cover their arms in white plastic bangles, from wrist to shoulder, perhaps to display some sort of status among themselves. The men wear the garb of poor herdsmen and farmers, the lungi, a tube-like piece of cloth that can be worn down as a long skirt, or, in hot weather, they tuck the hem up into the waist so that its length is scandalously above the knee. Although, this outer wear cannot be solely attributed to tribal culture, more just to hot weather and not enough money to buy western pants.

The tribal hamlets themselves are always located at a distance from the village. And this is merely those that have settled over the last twenty odd years. Most of the tribes keep animals, particularly goats or sheep, and some of them have lived nomadic lives always moving on to the next place with shrubs. Traditionally, when they have settled in the past, it was only long enough to grow a little food. Though now it seems that many tribal people have branched out into farming, or migrant farming, as they have a natural "knack" for the land.

Getting to Know the Tribal People

The tribal people in Andhra Pradesh came from the Northern states of India, from Rajastan, and from the deserts of the ancient kings. They migrated to the south and southeast. They are nomadic cattle herders, going from place to place seeking water and green pastures. Sometimes they would live on remote rock formations close to water sources.

When they came to Andhra Pradesh about thirty years ago, they were still nomads, but the government allotted them some lands to live on and raise fodder for their cattle. They were often discriminated against. People would say that the tribal people were not clean. It is true that the women might go two or three weeks without taking baths. They wear bangles—thick and white—and they would wear them from their wrists to their shoulders. They would rather keep them there than scrub up. So their hygienic habits were different from the village people, but they do not smell worse than the regular populace.

Their food habits are also different. People from the higher castes would cook their food thoroughly. Tribal people don't even cook their food most of the time. They like to eat raw vegetables and a hand-made bread called *roti*. They wear very colorful clothing and are proud of their customs, their music, dances, special holidays and their language. They don't always use rupees. They barter for what they need, trading work and maybe vegetables or goats. They are not Hindus or Muslims or Christians; they are animists. They worship snakes, stones, trees, and other things found in nature.

The tribal people have no castes as such, and they are not part of village caste systems. They do not participate in village rituals, marriages or other functions. They do not enter the houses of the villagers. There may be friendships and friendly ties with those in the village because of economic reasons. But they are a caste unto themselves. In the past they did not want the villagers to come into their colonies because they thought it would prevent them from preserving their culture.

The people from the untouchable caste live in the villages, but they live in very specific parts of the village. There are lines drawn through the village to separate different living areas for different caste levels. This practice is largely abandoned in the cities, but it is still seen in some local villages. So, even though tribal people are a caste unto themselves, it would not be acceptable for them to walk into an area that was designated to a higher caste.

We used to visit the tribal villages and ask them to share their music with us. I would learn to drum with them. We made many friends this way.

In those days there were no schools in the villages and many tribal children would go to work on farms. Some older boys would follow their fathers to the city to work in the construction business. So those who are left behind, mostly girls would take care of the little ones. The tribal people were very oriented to working. Their parents wanted them to earn a little money to improve their income. When we began the schools, we wanted to reach out to those who were being overlooked. There was an obvious need for these children to get an education, but we could not expect the children to be at school all day. The culture was not yet ready for that.

We would begin by teaching them the alphabet using things that made sense to their situation, drawing letters with sticks on the ground. We would teach them orally at first, saying the Telugu names of things they could see like cows, a bitter gourd, fruit, and those types of things. We would take them outside the village and show them different kinds of crops—lentils, rice, and vegetables. Those things they were going to need to know. Not long after we started, the government made a rule that each village should have a school. They began to send in teachers and to construct school buildings. When this came about, we welcomed the idea, but we asked, "What should we do now?"

Mission Partnerships Formed

We decided to start our own ministry. We called it VEDA. Those initials stand for Village Evangelism and Development Association. We began schools, a clinic for children, and provided courses for rural pastors.

In 1990 Doris and I attended the Mennonite World Conference in Winnipeg, and there we were surprised to meet David and Joanne Janzen. We had not seen them for fifteen years, although we had corresponded from time to time. We told them about our call from God to return to the rural areas where I grew up. Our vision was for a holistic ministry of evangelism, development, and for reconciliation among the tribal people and untouchables that we were getting to know. David and Joanne agreed to be mission partners with us, sharing our newsletters with friends in the States. These friends would send donations for our work through Reba Place Church in Evanston, Illinois, where the Janzens were now living in intentional community. Larry Kehler, from the Charleswood Mennonite Church in Winnipeg, agreed to be a mission partner for us in Canada. We had many Canadian friends because we had lived there for three years. We thank God that these partnerships have remained strong. David and Larry have both visited us in India.

I Could Help You with Your Refrigerator Problem

Joanne Janzen

Das visited us about ten years ago as he was touring the US and Canada to connect with supporters of their mission work in India. Das arrived just after we had returned from a summer trip with relatives in Kansas. Upon our arrival home, we discovered that our refrigerator had "died." We needed to toss most of the food we'd stored in it. We were sitting with Das on our back porch enjoying the

*summer evening and rehearsing what bad luck we'd had
with our refrigerator. Das responded to my long lament
by saying gently, "I could help you with your refrigerator
problem." Surprised, I asked, "Do you know how to fix
refrigerators?" With a slow smile he responded, "No, but I
could show you how to live without one."*

*The next day Das surprised us in another way. He
cooked a wonderful Indian meal of rice and curry, with
many side dishes, for a dozen friends at our dining room
table. The rice and all the other dishes came off the stove
at the same moment—and just on time—as the guests arrived. Then Das regaled us with stories of their work in
the schools and fledgling churches around Mallepalli and
Devarakonda.*

*It turns out that Das had been a single man long
enough to learn how to cook very well before Doris joined
him and took over the family kitchen. In his culture, he
said, it is a shameful thing for a man to be in the kitchen,
but he did not care about that. When Doris needed to
travel away from home, Das was glad he knew how to feed
their family.*

Joanne Janzen, along with her husband David, are communal
members of Reba Place Fellowship in Evanston, Illinois. They
try to keep up with two children and their spouses, along with
five grandchildren who live in New York, Pennsylvania, and
Evanston.

Bindu Home for Orphans and Bonded Laborers

Bindu means a drop, a drop of anything. It has no shape. It is
an insignificant drop of water or some other fluid. Our idea was
to take this drop, which has no shape or taste, and mold it into
something, something substantial.

The Bindu Home reaches out to children in the most desperate of circumstances. We wanted to recover children who were in bonded labor. Many untouchable families are so poor that they sell their boys, eight to twelve years of age, to local landlords to work as bonded laborers. They do this to get at least a bit of income for their family. The contracts are for one year, but this often becomes a lifetime of bondage because the families never get out of debt, so they can't pay for their children's release. I have a heart for the bonded laborers because this almost happened to me. My older brother had already been sold to a landlord, and my father was making arrangements to sell me when my aunt came from the city and arranged to have me put in a Mennonite Brethren orphanage.

In 1996, the first time we went out with this mission, we found two children. I would go and rescue children, buying or arranging for them to be set free. We formed the Bindu Home out of necessity because the children had to be put somewhere. Our Bindu family grew to twenty-seven children over the first three years. Most of them were of tribal or untouchable backgrounds. We also cared for some pastors' children so they could afford to go to school.

We thought it important to give the children some training. We started some boys in mechanical training; scooter mechanics and trade. They are good kids, but they don't have the means to go on to college. We want to give the children some hope when they leave the Home. Sometimes we can do that with training, or with an education that will get them a scholarship to college.

And then girls came and said that they also wanted to learn to do something that could earn them some money. So we started a sewing center. Noni Johnson, a young woman volunteer from the Woodcrest (Bruderhof) Community in New York came at that time and taught sewing. The Catskills's Community donated three sewing machines. That way the girls learned to sew and earn some money. Then other sewing machines were donated. The Shalom Sewing center still operates in Mallepalli.

Girls are particularly vulnerable in this culture. We give preference to girls, because they are the most neglected part of the family. Families in this culture think that a boy is a boon and a girl is a burden.

One girl in the Bindu Home has a very cruel father. After the birth of a daughter, he wanted a son to pass on the family line and insisted that they would have no more girls. When a daughter was born, he drowned her in the river. Three daughters perished in this way. When yet another daughter was born, his family begged him to at least let her live in the Bindu Home—which is what he did. Now he has a son and is happy, and visits his daughter from time to time.

Currently, there are 130 students living in the Bindu Home right next to our apartment. But times change, and every year brings with it new or different problems. The economic downturn in America has hurt us. Sponsors and supporters have withdrawn, which has left some of the students in difficult positions.

Our Calling among the People Where I Was Raised

My Mother

My mother died a long time ago
When I was too young to know
What it is to die or what it is to live?
These questions never entered my thoughts.
I was preoccupied with how to get a bowl of rice,
Or who would give it, cold or hot.
The other children, though poor as I,
Went home early while I played alone.
Now I have a child of my own whom I adore,
Named after her mother who is no more.
The village folk tease and tell me
I'm more like mother than ever she could be.

—Das Maddimadugu

Chapter 5

Enlarging the Tent of Compassion

Building Up Schools at Devarakonda and Mallepalli

GOVERNMENT SCHOOLS IN RURAL areas are free for all children. But they are not always accessible, and besides, they usually are terrible. A lot of money is allotted to education, but if you go to any school in the villages, you will find they are in the worst conditions. The classrooms don't have roofs. There are no benches, no toilets, no facilities. There are not adequate teachers, and the system is much neglected. The money allotted to the poor is amassed by government officials and ministers. The police, who are supposed to enforce the laws, are the most corrupt.

The private schools, especially Christian ones that remained after the British left, are known to provide good education because they do it for a cause and not for money. The Hindus and Muslims respect this and is why they send their children here.

In 1991 we took over a school in Devarakonda near the entrance of the village. It was small, with a small yard. The class rooms were like sheds with tin roofs and very hot. Then we began to receive funds from Harry Schmidt (a Canadian friend) and his family foundation, and we were able to buy some land on the edge of town, with a large yard for the children, and good facilities. We built up a primary school in Devarakonda for kindergarten through the first six grades that gives instruction to about 400 students.

In Mallepalli, where we live now, we have built up a larger school from kindergarten through high school that gives instruction to 1,000 children including 130 from the Bindu Home. For many years Doris was the superintendant of these schools, but now our son Nathan has taken charge. His college training was in computers. He has set up computer labs in our schools so that teachers and children learn how to use them and can prepare for the computer age.

Computer lab at the Malepalli school

Thanks Ma

Esther Maddimadugu,
as told to David Janzen: October 2010

I don't think I appreciated my mom until I came back from college. In fact I remember the precise moment this happened.

It was just another afternoon, the two of us drinking tea on the back steps. I don't remember what we were talking about or how it came up. But the conversation turned to Mom's life and about her work building up the Matilda schools. She told me about her days when the school had just started up and how busy she was. She would get up every morning at three or four o'clock, cook breakfast for us, pack our lunches for school. Then she would walk to the bus stop (about thirty minutes away), take a bus to the next station for another half hour, and then ride the bus for two to three hours to Devarakonda or Mallepalli. She would teach for half a day. After that she would spend another two to three hours on the bus back to the city with one more ride getting back home, and then she would make supper for us all. The next morning she would get up and do it all over again. I think she carried this heavy routine, traveling more than a hundred kilometers each way for a couple of years.

I was stunned. I don't think I had a clue. I have tried to pinpoint memories from that part of my life. But all I have are these vague and sometimes bitter recollections about having to take care of my brother and sister—give my brother a bath, take the both of them to school and back. But I never realized how much easier I had it because of my mom and what an example she set for the rest of us.

My mother built up the schools in Devarakonda and Mallepalli. My father had the vision, my mother made it happen.

Initially, when the school started, my mother was the only teacher with a kindergarten class. The first class was a one-room school in Mallepalli. Then they took over a school in Devarakonda that had come to an end. As the school added grades, Mother was the primary teacher and also the administrator who would hire and train other teachers. The teachers were English-educated, but they would lapse into Telegu, and she had would have to keep them on course to maintain an English-medium school.

At home, Mom had an envelope for everything that we would spend money on. Every paisha (smallest coin) she would keep track of. And she ran the school the same way. Mom did everything—taking charge of the finances, supplies, schedules—the day-to-day stuff that went on at school. My father was the public face of the school and dealt with parent contacts because he knew rural people in the area where he grew up and could relate easily in Telugu.

Back home in the city as an older sibling, I did what older siblings do. First I had to drop off the younger ones at their school and ride the bus forty-five minutes to my school, and I was often late. I would have been in middle school. But I did it. That is how it was for many others my age.

I was used to Mother being gone all day, so I noticed my dad's absences more. He made sure we got fed and cared for when she was gone. We always lived in Hyderabad. But more and more my parents would stay in Devarakonda for several days and come back over the weekend. When they were away a long time, like the trip to the Mennonite World Conference in 1990, my aunt would stay with us.

One reason our family did not move to the rural area is that my mom grew up in the city, so she felt more comfortable with us kids in the city where there were better schools.

My mother grew up in an English-speaking urban home. She learned how to speak the local Telugu slowly, and she only learned to read and write it when my brother Nathan was in school and she learned with him.

After I graduated from high school, I spent a year in the Devarakonda school as a teachers aid. Then I went to Canadian Mennonite Bible College. When I came back, I taught three years in the Devarakonda school. I filled in whatever grade they needed.

I remember in the afternoon, after the students went home, my mother and I would have tea together. Then we would go back to work for some more preparation. There was a room adjacent to the school where my parents often stayed. I had a room by myself at the end of the classroom row. Then one year I had a couple of other teachers who stayed with me.

When my parents were gone for a few months to North America, I was in charge, running the school. At that time there were about ten or twelve teachers in Devarakonda. The school was in an old rented building with wooden walls and a tin roof. In the summer it was very hot. Some rooms had fans and others not.

As a fellow teacher I could observe how my mother ran the school. Her communications would be direct and efficient. She did not beat around the bush. She had really high expectations of the teachers and the students. As an educator she knew what she was doing and was very good at it. The parents respected that kind of environment because they saw their kids were learning. Hers was a Western approach. She put people on the spot.

My dad had a more Indian approach. He was from that area and had many connections. He was the more relational person. He would remind Mother that people needed to save face. This was a difference of their approach, and the two usually worked together peaceably.

The expansion of the schools was my dad's idea and mom went along, administering more and more, taking the growing schools in stride. Mom found a mission in the schools. She did not have friends in the city because she was gone so often. In the village she had more relationships. But she did not want to move there permanently because of us children. She was a very busy person and did not hang out with friends very long.

When I was there in the Devarakonda school, I really enjoyed working with the kids, relating to them in and outside the classroom on a regular basis. In that sense I could say it was my mission. But in terms of the vision my dad had, it was too big for me. I was swept along and did my part.

Growing up, I knew that our family was different from other families around us. Explaining what my parents did was awkward. Other people did not understand why our family came back when we could have stayed in Canada or America.

I think that what my parents are doing is important. The vision has gotten big in some ways. I don't know that I would want to go back and continue it. I've learned a lot from being a part of it all, growing up and helping out when I was there. I appreciate it, and it taught me a lot.

In their marriage, my parents brought two worlds together. Us kids, we had the best and the worst of both. If it were not for my dad, we'd never have gone to the village. I have an appreciation for things both urban and things rural. I was able to see how important it was to be administratively on the ball and efficient like my mom, as well as having relationships with people that are close and genuine. They brought their own gifts to this. I've learned from both sides.

I know that my parents could have stayed abroad. My dad wanted to be in India, and my mom had a harder life because of it. As I sit here and think about all the things my mom has done—is doing—not only for us as a family, but in the years she poured into the schools, I am amazed at her strength and resilience, by her conscience and integrity. She was and is the one who held it all together. I don't think I could have or would have done what she did.

But I can say, "Thanks Ma."

~∽~

Esther Maddimadugu is married to Brent Graber. They live in Elkhart, Indiana, where Esther regularly works in the Elkhart schools as a substitute teacher, still filling in where needed. She appreciates the diversity of her students. She is an excellent Indian cook and loves to share rice, curry, and chai with guests and friends.

Whitey—It's Natural to be Ashamed

Julia Guyer: Journal

November 3, 2009: It will soon be too dark to write. I am sitting on the stairs that go up to the roof. The bugs are after me even though I am coated in Super Deet repellent. But it's worth it to see the sky turning from various blues to the reds and yellows of the setting sun. Every time I see the sunset, it is like I have never seen it before. All these people around our house are walking home. One regular sight is a lady leading her three water buffalo right by our house around sunrise and then back again at sunset. She seems too old to handle three full-sized cows, but I guess that is a difference here. Work is always just happening all around us. There are no exceptions.

Today I taught at the Matilda school from eight-thirty am until three-thirty pm. Back in the States that would be a full day of work, more than I feel like I've done in a while. Here that is only a half day of work. The other teachers are always there before me and they go home after I do. And there is no Saturday off. Apparently that is another "American tradition." The teachers that live next door to us work from eight am to six pm. And then when they finish dinner, they return to school to do tutorials until nine pm. I do not understand all this work. It's like there is more work than there are people to do it, but that doesn't make sense considering the population of India. There are definitely enough people for the work, many of them desperately needing employment.

Being here makes me feel lazy. All the Indian people in my peer group work really long days at the school, and we, the privileged creamy whitey-whites only work half the day and half the week. And worse, compared to the jobs I had back in the states, this is even more work than I usually do. I live a life of comfort and leisure, at a very low cost. Gaining this awareness is good for me, but I find myself disagreeing with myself about it throughout the day. Come on, let's be realistic, I like leaving the school at three pm. I don't want to stay until six pm, come home for an hour and go back until nightfall. The difficult question here is, what does this mean about me? What kind of person am I really?

We have an open sewer in our backyard where children, and some adults, "go to the bathroom" in the bushes or in plain sight all the time. Here is a daily sample of the constant flow of human life on this planet. Here the truth is in your face; the waste does not disappear. Here, what kind of person am I?

I have been thrown into a vortex which calls everything about me and "my world" into question. Right now my being is squirming, and I can't stand myself.

The way I work and leisure, eat and dispose, and even drink magnify every irony of my life. For example: we buy our drinking water. I am somewhat terrified of getting sick from the water. Andrea would drink it (and probably does), but I did that once when I went to Central America and got so ill the village people nearly took me to the doctor in a wheelbarrow. I feel terrified to the point of paranoia. I can't help but wonder if even the rainwater is contaminated. So we purchase our drinking water in giant cooler bottles from a company called "Kinley." Don't let the name fool you, it's just a subsidiary of the Coca-Cola company, internationally known for its corporate imperialism. So I come here, not only knowing all this, but also feeling angry about it. I use this purchased water even for cooking because of how fear has gripped me. I am revolting.

I am supposed to be teaching English to children who do not speak it natively. They are expected to learn it because in India this is what is it means to get a "good" education. How much can I rant in one journal entry about American imperialism, or how much I am contributing to it by being here? My mother's voice in my head is saying, "Well, Julia, the Indians don't seem to mind. This is what they want." I am not convinced though, and very confused. If I have the least fidelity to what I have discovered to be the truth, then I must argue firmly against what I am doing.

I am being made painfully aware of all my freedoms, which of course I take for granted just like we take our mothers for granted. Some freedoms have been there for me since I can remember. They are unalienable, right?

I came to India to have my eyes opened. My attempt to teach feels preposterous. I came here to learn. How do I explain to others that I have come because there are many things that only India can teach me? Can it be that these children will lead me out of the cave into which I was born? A cave which told me I was free, but denied me reality.

I was outside just now, doing laundry, my hands in the bucket of soapy water with my clothes. And I looked up into the sky above me and it was beautiful. The same sky that seems to watch me in all the places I've ever called home. It is true that washing your clothes by hand under this blue India sky is a good thing. It is significant.

There is so much good here. And I am asking India— the voice of India in its children—to open my eyes to what is truly good. It seems to be a wholesome good. I might not know what I am asking for, but I want that pearl of great price. I would give up all the freedoms I have known for this one more beautiful than all the rest. Simplicity is a freedom I know so little about.

A Farm at Angadipet

We were able to buy a ten acre farm near my home village of Angadipet. My brother managed it for me until he died in 2005. With his help we dug an irrigation well that allowed for two crops a year. The farm grew rice for the Bindu home, sweet limes for sale, and other food for our needs. We began to experiment with progressive farming techniques and would host demonstration seminars with agricultural extension agents for the benefit of farmers in the area.

A Visit to the Farm

David Janzen: Journal

November 15, 2007: The approach road had a big bump the car could not cross, so we had to walk half a mile to the farm. Das warned me about cobras, but we didn't see any.

I am impressed by how much Das has invested in the farm, both materially and of himself. There is a sweet lime orchard, an irrigation well, a system of underground pipes with economical drip irrigation, coconut trees, a flock of sheep, water buffaloes, oxen, and more. The rice grown here, now ready for harvest, feeds the Bindu Home children for about three months of the year. I also sense from Das how deeply he feels about the land—a different kind of investment. Though Das has not lived on the land, his older brother farmed it for him, and this made it home. Since his brother's death, undependable help has robbed some of Das's joy in the place. But now, it seems, he has a farmer who looks after things in an interested and dependable way, and Das is happy to see the results. This farm is the source of much of the food and some milk for Bindu Home children.

The farmer took us around and showed us the land. I was especially impressed to see the thirty-foot-deep well, not a bore well, but a huge block of earth and rock excavated to make a hole as big as an underground house. Das and his brother worked for six months to dig it, with picks and dynamite, plus some occasional help from a back hoe. The well water it provides could be enough to irrigate the whole ten acres, but there is only enough electricity available to irrigate about half of it. The rest grows vegetables in the monsoon season. We toured the rice paddies, golden ripe and ready for the harvesters coming the next day.

While I was present with a camera, the farmer rounded up his team of oxen and hitched them to a plow so I could take his picture. Then his wife ran to join him behind the oxen: she had put on her best sari. I must remember to send them the photo

Farmer with wife and oxen.

But most, I want to remember the way Das relaxed after lunch at the home of his deceased brother's widow, telling stories about growing up as a Dalit (untouchable) in the 1940's. He remembers going out as a small boy, guiding his blind father for days of begging. People would give them food, and they would sit under a tree where his father, a man known for gentleness, would share with him half-and-half, and they'd eat the food together. He felt no shame in begging while with his father, though the other children would taunt him for it.

I asked how Dalits were treated in those days. "It was expected," Das said, "that Dalits were servants of everyone in the village on the other side of the road and there was no compensation for the service. They would sweep the streets and yards of houses, only never go past the threshold. They were never welcome at weddings or other public events where food was shared. Only at harvest time, they could go to the rice fields, and a portion of the harvest was dealt out to them to live on for the year. They were expected to take away all dead animals and bury the dead at funerals. They were considered "unclean" and not allowed to touch anyone of another caste. Others could own property, go to school or enter the trades, but not the untouchables."

I could not help but wonder what would be the loss for the world if the good news of Jesus, embodied in the love of a few Christians, had not gotten to Das, and he had remained an indentured servant, stuck behind a team of water buffalo for the rest of his life.

Planting and Supporting Churches

I felt very strongly about helping people the way I was helped, not just with schools, but with the church as well. When the missionaries came to the villages, they declared three things: that people needed hospitals, schools, and churches. I remember as a child that even if there was not a church close by in the village, it would be made available at a central location and all would go there. We had started work with the children, but we also wanted to have a church.

Our first church began in Devarakonda in a neighborhood that had a terrible reputation. These were Untouchables, and the men were stone cutters. Their work was brutally hard. The men would work till the heat of the day and then take their earnings to a local bar and drink it all away. The women had nothing with which to feed the children and would prowl the streets as prostitutes to make a living. Violent quarrels often erupted. There were no government programs, social services, or other employment for the women.

When my brother and I went there we saw boys ten or eleven years old wearing no clothes in the daytime when other children would be at school. We asked why the children were not in school. They said "Why should the children go to school to cut stones. We are better stone cutters than those who go to school." So I went with a Christian teacher and hired a small room. The lady would collect some children—little ones. She would take a pail of water and wash them up, then teach the alphabet and little songs by repetition. When we asked the parents to provide slates and chalk they answered, "Why should we? It's your school." So we bought some sand and spread it on the floor and scratched numbers and letters for the children to read. For one year we did that.

Then some teenage girls started coming to watch. One day Noni Johnson, a nineteen-year-old Bruderhof volunteer, went with us. The teenage girls were so curious to see a white woman. Noni taught 'Jesus loves me' and other songs. She drew animals on paper. The girls loved her. They asked if she could teach them to sew some shirts. Noni's mother's community sent money to buy three sewing machines. The girls began to come for sewing lessons, some of them fourteen years old and pregnant.

The Gift of Empathy

Noni Johnson: October 2010

I remember going with Das to the Stonecutter Anjiah Colony Church. There were up to eighty people in this small room—mostly women, girls, and children. At least a dozen were teenage girls with their babies. Das translated as they asked for help in learning a trade. These girls' husbands had gone to the cities in search of work, to become something other than stone cutters all their lives—and I don't blame them. Unfortunately, that left these teenage mothers with no source of income, no way to feed themselves or their children. They resorted to prostitution as the only way they knew to survive. I, who had a chance for an education to learn so many skills, realized that these girls had none of that. All it would take would be fifty dollars to buy a sewing machine: then they could learn to sew and earn money with dignity.

First meeting place of the Stonecutter's Church.

My mother asked the Catskill Bruderhof to send some money. When the two sewing machines arrived, they were treadle-powered because electricity is so sporadic. Das, Doris, and I took the machines to the church and set them up. The girls had brought garlands of marigolds and jasmine which they put around our necks. They wanted me to be the first one to sew on the machines, but I had never used a treadle machine, and just made a big tangle. But the eagerness and excitement on these girls' faces is something I will never forget. Their hope of rising above desperate poverty—it's a feeling that I, who have never lived in poverty without escape, cannot really understand.

We hired a man and his wife to teach them. I had first thought I should get patterns, but that is not how it's done in India. The garment-maker just looks at you and somehow the clothes end up a perfect fit.

In this same colony, Das started building a larger church meetinghouse because the one we used was too small and more people were coming. Das always had these visions of where he wanted to build a church or school, but never the funds. That didn't stop the visions though, even when some months we were short on the teachers' salaries. Das always found ways—sometimes selling small pieces of his land or his family going without things they needed.

If a student's family didn't have money to pay the month's tuition, they'd arrange something with Das. One child's father made benches, as he was a carpenter. One father brought rice. One time the rice came at the perfect time, too, as there wasn't enough money for the teachers' salaries. The teachers living in the school had run out of food—and then, there came the rice right on the day when we did not know what we'd have to eat in the evening.

In the evenings we'd sometimes go to the tribal villages, and the people would sing and dance for us. Das would try to connect with the children and would ask them if they knew their alphabet. He'd write with a stick in the dusty roads. If the kids weren't going to school, he'd try to convince the parents that they needed school. He'd hire teachers to do evening classes for the children whose families depended on their work for survival—usually herding the goats, water buffaloes, or whatever work they had.

Das would point to a tree and say "That is the school." The children would all sit in the shade of that tree. I thought, "Can't you at least imagine school being a thatched roof to keep out the rain and walls against the wind?" But that is how the visions grew.

Das cared for the teachers like a father. He'd try to make outings or field trips for us to have some fun. One time he took us to a government guest house by a beautiful lake and an orange grove where we all spent the day and had a picnic. Or we'd hike up the fort overlooking Devarakonda, or visit his farm which, at the time, wasn't producing anything.

On evenings when Das and Doris were in Devarakonda, we'd have dinner together and devotions, and then end up singing for hours, teaching each other songs and singing hymns in two and three-part harmony, which to the other teachers was a new idea. Then the teachers would teach us their songs in Malyalam.

One teacher was from a very poor family on the coast. She was her family's only hope of rising up out of their desperate poverty. Sadly, we had some problems with her at school, but Das had such a heart and understanding of what she meant to her family. He wanted to make sure they were provided for even when all the rest of us were fed up with her decisions. He said he could not fire her with a good conscience knowing how it would affect her family.

One time we had no money for gas for the school jeep which picked up the students. The teachers who lived in the school had to forgo their salaries that month and Das used the money for his bus ticket back to Hyderabad to *pay for fuel. I also remember Das accompanying to the hospital a student who had a severely deformed leg due to polio so the boy could have reconstructive surgery on it.*

Das reminds me of the Good Samaritan who, when he saw a need, responded to it, not worrying about how it would affect him, but rather what would happen to the persons if he didn't act. He knew suffering and being deprived. He could understand and feel it all with the people. God had given him the gift of empathy, and he used it to bring others to Jesus.

Noni Johnson came to India in 1995 as a nineteen-year-old volunteer from the Catskill Bruderhof. After rereading her letters to her family from that time away from home, she wrote these memories in October, 2010.

Why Do You Come?

Then the village people began to ask, "Why do you come?" So we told them about Jesus' love, and we began a house fellowship in the same room. Perhaps fifteen came. Our daughter Esther came along. After two years a church was born. Then local people began to come from beyond the stone cutters neighborhood. An old lady came and did all the action songs with so much vigor. She asked us "Why don't you get a bigger place?" We were often forty people in a little room. She offered us the land where the new church has now been built. She also insisted on paying the title registration. The site on top of a rocky hill is significant for the Christians because Hindus and Muslims also try to claim hilltops for mosques and temples.

One day Harry Schmidt came to visit from Canada. He could not pass through the crowd of people in that small room to get to the front. After he went home, he began sending money for a little church on the rock. I talked to the stone cutters.

They offered, after their day of work, instead of drinking, they would cut stones for the foundation. We asked the neighborhood to raise 10,000 rupees as seed money. The men said what they earned was only enough for drinking, no extra. But they volunteered hours to dig the foundation, cut stones, and a mason offered his services. I felt that God did not want a small church here but a large one,

We laid out the walls about 40 by 60 feet. We wanted this to be a center for surrounding villages. The money Harry Schmidt sent was enough for the cement. The folks from the Taiwan International Church and Reba also contributed, and we raised the walls up to the roof.

Then the BJP (Hindu nationalist party) came and told us to stop. You are making too much noise. It is illegal to build a church on this site," they said. The BJP youth threatened the people who came to church.

New Shalom Ashram (stone cutters)
meeting house in Devarakonda.

I appointed Devapriyam as pastor. He was a former criminal, a thug who killed people for pay before he became a Mennonite Christian. His wife was a Christian and prayed for him for six years. One time he threw a crowbar that went through her side. After his conversion, he became a good pastor, but he still reacted too strongly at times.

Several times we appealed to the government for legal permission to proceed and were denied because the BJP kept threatening the officials. Finally a higher-up in the district government told us they had nothing against our work and that we could finish the roof, so we did. Now, since 2005, the Congress Party is in power, and the climate is more favorable for minorities; there is respect for civil rights.

The church attracts college students and people from the neighboring villages. The original stone cutter people stopped coming when BJP made their threats. Now some have returned. Their children come to Sunday school. But the neighborhood has been transformed. Now children go to school. The women have employment in sewing and other work—no prostitution. The men are present to their families. The neighborhood used to be dangerous and no one dared pass through at night. Now, one is welcomed.

Shalom Ashram congregation at worship.

The new pastor, Ratnam and his wife Shoba are leading the congregation well. Ratnam was an independent who has two years of pastoral training. He has a big voice and leads singing well, is charismatic and prays for healing. The church has a reputation for giving. The offerings include jewelry, rice, firewood—whatever people have.

Witnessing to Our Faith

David Janzen: Journal

November 15, 2007: Das talked about their freedom and their limits in sharing the content of Christian faith. "When we work in the schools and other social projects, we labor side-by-side with non-Christians and can come close to them. We can share our faith and people are not so rigid in opposing this. In school we are expected to teach 'Morals' as a subject, and there we can tell about Jesus. Hindus have no problem learning about one more holy being, and Muslims also have a place for Jesus in their beliefs. In our sewing centers we can read the Bible and teach simple songs."

But Das feels the heart of his ministry these days is his relationship with twenty-two pastors in the area. Three receive full-time salaries from Matilda Educational Society, and the others get smaller allowances, help with their children's school fees, or bicycles that enable them to reach neighboring villages. Together they have made evangelistic visits to 100 villages in the past eighteen months. The lead church in this network is the Shalom Ashram (Stone Cutters) Church in Devarakonda, where Ratnam and his wife Shoba are the pastoral team. Two churches, where pastors Simonu and Adam lead, have permanent buildings under construction.

This morning, Das and I rode out by motor scooter to visit a half-built meetinghouse in Gajinagar, a little village ten km away. It was a tricky ride in that Das was learning how to manage a new scooter, and I was learning to relax in the seat behind him. As he gained skill and confidence, I learned my part, too—a little. The pastor, Adam, was not at home, but his mother welcomed us and showed us around. Das explained how a pastor must be in place serving a congregation faithfully for five years, and then Das tries to gather the funds to build a permanent meeting house. This one is about 25 by 40 feet. It still needs trusses and a roof. The government donated the site, which is large enough for a pastor's house and a small informal school that is yet to come. The people already meet in the building despite its unfinished condition with sand floor and a pile of bricks in the corner.

Das at unfinished Gajinagar church meeting house

How shall I tell about the church service at the village of Gajinagar this evening with about twenty Dalits and a few tribal people worshipping together in a half-finished meeting house with no roof, open to the moon and the stars?

Actually, I must begin with a walking tour of the village that has two castes, dalits and shepherds. Cows and sheep were coming home at dusk, as well as a few school children walking from Devarakonda, five kilometers away. We waited by the village turnoff from the small highway as night was falling. I was surrounded by a dozen kids jostling to get close, eager to make eye contact with me. I showed them the three or four magic tricks I had, taught them how to play patty cake, and was quickly at the end of my repertoire, so I took pictures of them in goofy poses and showed them what they looked like in the digital monitor. One fifth grade boy knew a little English—the pastor's son—and would translate for us.

Then four drummers arrived and built a little fire of twigs to heat up (tune) their drums to a higher pitch. Das and I were regaled with festive turbans and garlands of flowers. Then with drums beating, we processed in parade from the highway an eighth of a mile to the meetinghouse. The tribal women, with a hundred bangles on each arm and sparking little mirrors glinting in their dresses, sang and danced jubilantly with upraised hands, moving before Das, me and the rest of the crowd on our way to the meetinghouse. I think the idea was to make a spectacle that might attract non-Christians to see what is going on, but also to express their joy at visitors coming from afar and their unity in Jesus.

As we arrived in the meetinghouse, the pastor and a few other men were hastily rigging up one light attached to a tall stick leaning against a corner. The pastor was tearing off insulation from wires with his teeth and twisting live wires together until the bulb shone brightly and the speaker system worked—sort of. We were not a big crowd, but it is important for the whole village to hear that something is going on at the meetinghouse. After a time of chorus singing with lots of clapping, I was asked to give a speech as Das translated.

I told the story of friendship our family has been given with Das and Doris, and why I had come to see the work God has called them to do among the people of Andhra Pradesh. I also talked about the call to peacemaking from a God whose love extends not just to us, or to people like us, or to people different from us, but even to our enemies. We are a people of peace with a mission of reconciliation. Das, of course, extended my talk with his translation, adding whatever else the Spirit gave him to say.

I thought that would be "it," but then three women came forward requesting me to pray for healing for them or their families, and while they knelt three others came, and then two more. So I prayed for them in English whatever the Spirit gave me to say, holding my hand on the head of each one in turn. I felt the power of their faith and trust in God, and in me as God's servant. Then as we went out to the car, two more women asked me for prayer, and one more. Several of the women blessed me in return by bowing with hands held together till their heads touched the ground, or holding my hands as we walked, or taking my hands and kissing them. I did not expect to come this close to people with whom I share no language, but it is clear we are united in Jesus, a Jesus who has shown them overflowing love that they are privileged to pass on.

Pastoral Seminars

From time to time we have been able to host seminars and conferences for area pastors and their wives who often have little formal education. We bring in speakers from the U.S., Canada, Taiwan, and from India as well. They have taught the biblical basis of peacemaking, marriage enrichment, and how to study the Bible.

I remember a visit from Don Jacobs, Director of Mennonite Leadership Foundation who taught about Paul's three missionary journeys. Melvin Loewen, formerly from the World Bank, Congo, put together the Bible with economics, showing how businesses can support church growth. We visited some Christian business enterprises in the city to hear how the faithful help plant new churches with the money they earn themselves. That created many new ideas for our pastors. Each year we bring together several hundred pastors in seminars that create tremendous bonds of fellowship.

But I remember most fondly going out in teams of evangelists, visiting villages for a week at a time. We would teach the children songs and they would sing with us till midnight. Often the tribal women went around dancing to the folk songs. We enacted dramas, told Bible stories, and made people think. Eating the simple food served on leaves, sleeping under the open skies, and taking baths in a communal well was such a delight for me. It brought back my childhood days. And the most joyous thing was to tell the children in the villages that Jesus loves them, that He sets slaves and bonded laborers free, and that He can help them learn to read and write in our informal village schools, that they all have value in his eyes.

An Ecumenical Seminar for Church Leaders

Don Jacobs: September 2010

Hyderabad, VEDA, Deverakonda, Matilda, Mallepalli, stone cutters, indentured boys, school children in colorful uniforms standing in rows. For me this is a new, exciting but strange world. Central India.

There I sit among pastors of all denominations, who have left their shoes at the door. They are singing monotonal hymns of praise to God as stringed instruments carry a tune. The music is strange to my ears. I am used to harmony and movement, more sprightly singing, may I say. But I was aware of the fact that their hymns focused on the One called Jesus in whose name we met and under whose Spirit we were together. Our host and hostess, sitting with us, translated the lyrics, all of which followed familiar themes. So, instead of fussing about the strangeness of the music, I praised God for the privilege of sitting with our friends Das and Doris Maddimadugu as a warm Indian breeze blew across our eager faces. The seminar for church leaders was about to begin. I bathed in the charm of the moment. Even the music sounded more friendly as the verses were repeated!

Anna Ruth and I were humbled as we sat among the pastors and deacons and spouses under a temporary shelter in the schoolyard where Das and Doris ran a school for local children. Every year they invite all the church leaders of the region, of all denominations, to come together for fellowship and leadership development training. I had the rare privilege of being among the teachers that year.

Near the town of Devarakonda, on a hill, stand the remains of an ancient stone castle, once home to Islamic rulers who filled their treasury with money from their enormously prosperous diamond trade. Some of the world's most costly diamonds came from there. The once glorious castle is now derelict. We saw goats and sheep grazing among the walls of the roofless ruins, a silent reminder of an era, now past, when Muslims, not Hindus, ruled the area.

As the Islamic era faded, Hindus stepped in alongside the remaining Muslims and slowly gained dominance. Among the Hindus and the Muslims were people who had no "Hindu blood," people who maintained a traditional religion. They had no place in Hindu or Islamic *communities. As "outsiders" they were treated as such. Our friend, Das, was born as one of them.*

I think I first met Das at the Overseas Ministry Study Center, where I heard his story—an arresting tale if there ever was one. Having climbed out of his tribal milieu as a believer in Jesus Christ, he tasted the good things of a new life, but apart from his own people. In due time the Spirit of God upset his personal plans and sent him back to serve not only his own people, but all who lived in the Devarakonda area. Their story touched me deeply and I wanted to know more of this man and woman of God, Das and Doris.

So, I am sitting with them at the Pastors' Conference in Devarakonda. I tried my best to sing bits and pieces of the songs the church leaders were singing under that temporary tent. Unsuccessfully, of course. Notwithstanding, my heart melted with praise and thanksgiving. Here I sat, part of the amazing ministry of these remarkable people. They are Mennonites, to be sure, Anabaptist to the core, but their hearts set no limits on the Body of Christ. Just look who is here! Men, women, young leaders, some from denominations that I knew about, some new ones. All these leaders respect Das highly, as is quite evident, and I am sure they are truly thankful that at least once a year they can participate in a Christian Leadership Seminar. I admire Das for providing this opportunity. It expresses his desire to unify the believers and to upgrade the leadership of all the groups.

Today, in an era dominated by Hindu and Islamic influence and power, the Christian community is small and scattered. In order to build up the faith community, Das established this annual training event where leaders of the groups of believers can tell their stories, share their joys and grief, and leave knowing that they have brothers and sisters throughout the region. They are all part of the Kingdom of Jesus Christ. I marveled at the wisdom that fashioned this ministry of love, reconciliation and discipleship—largely the vision God gave to Das. The vision became a reality, and I, praise God, sit humbly and thankfully among them.

Most of my life was given to help Western missionaries better understand their calling and the challenges that always go with cross-cultural ministries. That did not apply to Das and Doris. No, they are writing a new chapter, a new "book," in fact, which describes the pain, pathos, joy, and exhilaration of taking the Gospel of the grace of God in Jesus to a context where one's own life was shaped. I speak specifically of Das, a son of "untouchables." For Doris, it calls for every grace within her to wholly plunge herself into this ministry that embraces the realities of a broken, but hopeful, community.

Jesus is building his church. The believers in this area are joining the swelling chorus of those around the world who have been captured by the love of God in Christ Jesus. They add their voices to the choir that blends all songs into a hymn of praise. It is the sweet sound of thanksgiving rising from the souls of men and women of every tribe and nation on earth, all lauding the Lamb of God.

I try to catch the tune as the Indian music moves deliberately along its one line of melody, up and down, now loud, now soft. I try to absorb the unfamiliar. Without realizing, it I find myself humming a bass part that I imagine can and maybe should be there. "Hush," I say to myself. "Add nothing but praise and thanksgiving. It is their song, you have yours. Both exalt Jesus Christ, God's Lamb. Sit still and worship."

~∼∼

Don Jacobs was the Director of Mennonite Christian Leadership Foundation, established to encourage churches in the training and development of effective Christian leaders. The Annual Leadership Seminar that Das directed fit this description nicely.

Threats of Persecution

A few years ago in our region there were communists who would kill rich people and burn their houses. They were anti-government and anti-rich. Near our old place in Devarakonda we had a neighbor with some big construction cranes, and these radicals put bombs in them and blew up his cranes. They began to kill local politicians so the remaining government officials fled to Hyderabad.

We started to receive threats from someone claiming to be part of this radical group. He wasn't actually part of it, but he wanted money. We continued to do what we were doing, and we ignored him.

Every year we have a Christmas campfire program and the parents of our school children come. There were about 500 people there a few years ago. We hosted a candle-light service, and after it ended, people came up to me and told me that there were radicals at the program watching us. That was scary—to think that they were inside the gates of the school. But we were not doing anything wrong. I believe that if they wanted to kill us, they would have done it by now. So there was nothing to be afraid of. But I think that, ultimately, the radicals knew what we were about. They know everything about everyone. They knew that we are only trying to help the children, so that entire time they did not bother us.

In more recent times we have been harassed by Hindu Nationalists who want to resist all non-Hindu influences. They have forced us to close school on certain occasions and beaten some of our teachers. Sometimes they have demanded that we send our children to their propaganda rallies under threat of violence. Radical Hindu Nationalists are offended by Christians, Muslims, and Hindus working together.

In the winter of 2009 there was a great deal of agitation by student organizations and other politicians who want to break apart the state of Andhra Pradesh to create Telangana—a state

just for Telugu-speaking people. They declared strikes that forced
us to close the school during twenty days of normal operation.
Students' parents had to close their shops because of strikes and
threats of violence, so it was difficult for everyone to pay their bills.

No Choice But to Do the Work
God Has Given Us to Do

Jeannie Stuckey, as told to David Janzen: October 2010

*Back in the States, Das and Doris visited us at least three
times over the years. The first time is memorable because
their children gave ours the chickenpox. We also met Das
and Doris at the Mennonite World Conference in 1990,
where Das gave several presentations of their work.*

*When their daughter, Esther, wanted to attend the
Associated Mennonite Biblical Seminaries in Elkhart IN
where we live, Das and Doris asked us to be her sponsor,
which we were happy to do. She lived with us until she
could move into the dormitory. At the time of Esther and
Brent Graber's wedding, we celebrated with Das and Doris
at the outdoor ceremony on the seminary grounds, and
then went inside for the Indian meal. It was a joyful time
together.*

*In 2006 we went to India for a two week Rotary
International-sponsored polio eradication tour, and then
we visited Das and Doris for another week. I remember
how hospitable Doris was in preparing our meals. With
a helper, they were squatting on the kitchen floor with
cutting boards, preparing food in the Indian fashion. And
then we would sit on the cool floor in the incredibly hot
air, eating with our fingers, and hearing stories of their life.*

*I remember trips we took with them. We spent much
of that time at the two schools. They were digging a well*

for the new school in Devarakonda. There was not yet a wall around the compound at Mallepalli and Das was concerned about cobras getting into the children's quarters. The Grace Clinic was newly inaugurated. We went to the sewing project where the women were learning to use sewing machines for a livelihood.

One evening we went into the countryside to visit a night school. They had the children formally greet us and go through their routine of reciting their readings. Then some tribal women performed a dance for us in their elaborate garb, maybe five of them with music. It was so infectious that I started dancing with them. Everyone took pictures of the fun and joy we had together.

We slept in Das and Doris's apartment in Mallepalli. It was just the beginning of the hot season when the temperature would climb to 120 degrees Fahrenheit. Allen would lay on the floor with an electric fan just to cool off. The wells were running dry and everyone had to buy water from tanker trucks.

I remember some serious-looking men who came to talk with Das under a tree. Later we asked him about it. That was a time when some local people were threatening him because he had connections with Americans. They were trying to extort money from him. Yes, this was frightening. He told them he had no choice but to go on and do the work that God had given him to do. I remember praying with and for them, leaving them in the heat, in the shortage of water, and dealing with threatening extortionists. Talking about it does not give a sense of being there with them. It really brought home the kind of conditions they live in and helped us remember to pray for them.

I am struck now by the change in Das over the years. When we first knew him he was this slender "happy go lucky guy." Now we see him carrying the responsibility for many people and the weight of opposition he has faced.

The kinds of ministries they have going are incredible—the things they oversee together. But we also remember the joy Das and Doris had in taking us to meet new people and telling their stories. There is a quiet pride in showing us all the things they have brought to life with the help of God.

Jeannie Stuckey, with her husband Dr. Allen Stuckey, live in Elkhart IN. They served with the Mennonite Central Committee in Vietnam from 1969 to 1972. Jeannie finds joy in sponsoring a Bindu Home child.

A Crisis is Brewing

David Janzen: Journal

November 12, 2007: A crisis is brewing this morning. Just as the school day was to begin, the headmistress and a teacher came to Das and Doris' door to confer about an urgent matter. Word had just arrived from the radical Hindu Student Union that all schools in Andhra Pradesh are to be closed today. Nathan has just arrived from his weekend in Hyderabad and is calling the principal of the school in Devarakonda to put all the children back on the buses and send them home, but to keep the teachers for a meeting

I continued talking with Nathan, who explained that last week, in a Catholic school nearby, the principal asked a certain student to take off his Hindu tie and wear the school uniform like everyone else. A radical Hindu student group learned of the episode and invaded the school, beat up some teachers and ransacked the school central office. The next day the same group came here to the Matilda school and demanded that it close. One of the staff members was knocked to the ground and kicked around until other teachers pulled him away.

There is no use calling the police at times like this because they have a Hindu majority and, according to Nathan, "are worse than the radical students. The Hindu radicals pick on Catholics and other Christian groups. They leave Muslims alone because they will violently retaliate," Nathan explains.

There has been a Hindu nationalist movement in India since colonial times. It believes that the Hindu majority deserves to live in a Hindu state just like Pakistan, which was created for Muslims and like Israel for the Jews. On the other hand, the Congress Party of Gandhi, Nehru, and Indira Gandhi, has promoted the vision of a secular government that allows all religious groups to flourish in tolerance of each other.

Gandhi was assassinated by a radical Hindu nationalist who believed the leader for independence had failed the Hindu cause. For other Hindus, the movement is not so much about asserting Hindu nationalism as expressing a revitalization of Hinduism for a modern context. The Bharatiya Janata Party (BJP), representing Hindu aspirations, has played second place to the Congress Party through most of independent India's history, but did come into power nationally from 2000 to 2005, and now is in second place again in the national government with the Congress Party at the helm

Nevertheless, the radical Hindu student groups have gained a lot of influence through militant organizing of Hindu youth, with violence and threats of more violence. No authorities seem willing to confront them because they all—police and political parties, too—have Hindu sympathizers in their ranks

~~~

November 14, 2007: Today the Hindu student group is holding a rally in Mallepalli. They have sent word that all school children must attend. Such communications are made most politely, but threats of violence are implicitly understood. Das proposes that the Mallepalli school will comply to the extent of taking the upper classes with a few teachers to the rally, and then will talk about the experience afterwards

I think of the need for Christians here in India to be involved in schools, clinics, and other services that benefit everyone, not just Christians. Christians might argue, "Why not concentrate just on planting churches, pastoral training—spiritual things. Wouldn't that produce the greater return—rather than schools for mostly Muslim and Hindu children? They learn to sing Christian choruses, but almost never become Christians as adults."

One answer in this context is that these visible social services are what it takes to gain permission to live as Christians among a pagan majority. Many people here would like to kick the Christians out of India, except, "the Christians have better schools, and that's where you want to send your kids." So you don't kick them out, at least not till your kids graduate. Furthermore, a great number of the politicians have been trained in Christian schools, so they also have a certain loyalty and gratitude despite their populist rhetoric for Hindu interests.

Das also spoke about their schools and the Bindu Home, as islands of peace and cooperation between Hindus, Muslims and Christians. That is a witness to a surrounding society, where Hindus and Muslims are mistrustful of each other, where friendships across that boundary are rare and "incidents" can escalate quickly. Community built around doing the things Jesus taught can work between people of different backgrounds. "This is what India needs," Das says.

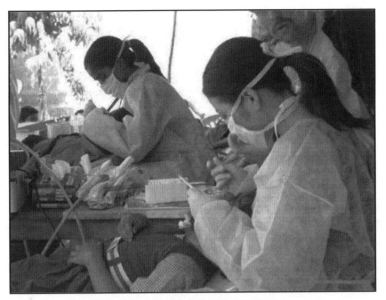

**Taipei International Church dental team
caring for Matilda school students.**

Helping Others as We Have Been Helped

About ten years ago we began to restructure our finances to meet Indian law. We formed a new non-profit organization called the Matilda Educational Society. (Matilda is Doris' maiden name.) We were granted a tax number that allows us to receive foreign donations. We are required to turn in quarterly financial reports and an audited report each year. The schools are the main recipient of donations, but we are allowed to do other work like flood relief, and retreats for pastors of churches in our area

We have had a relationship with the Taipei International Church in Taiwan. Many years the TIC has sponsored a dental team or a medical team to visit. In 2008 their dental team held a camp where six dentists and six technicians and six members of the TIC congregation came. They provided dental fillings, extractions, and teeth cleaning. They also conducted hygiene classes in our Matilda schools to demonstrate how to brush teeth and take care of gums. They distributed 1,300 toothbrushes to our students. A doctor also came instructing on diets that are healthy. They did all this in a Christian spirit and shared their personal testimonies. About 5,000 patients, including children from various schools came to take advantage of this camp.

Taipei International Church Partners with Matilda Education Society

Gerry Cooper

Our Taipei International Church (TIC) connection to Pastor Das dates back to 1997 when our then Mennonite pastor, Nathan Showalter, gave me a Mennonite Missions monthly magazine to peruse just as our Missions Committee, on which I was a new member, was looking for some Asian-based ministries to support. I began corresponding by letter with Das about his many-faceted V.E.D.A. Ministries and invited him to visit our church.

Das and Doris spent several days with us in 1998, on their way to a Missions Conference in New Haven, CT. At that time, we came to know his story and his heart for missions. We learned that this orphan from the untouchable caste, had been raised by two Canadian Mennonite missionaries. We learned of his education in Winnipeg, his service with Doris in Vietnam, his airlifting orphaned babies out of Saigon just before the fall of the city, his subsequent commitment to return with Doris to serve the Lord among his Muslim and Hindu countrymen in the very same impoverished villages in the Nalgonda District from which he had come, and his desire to give boys and girls an opportunity to escape from the caste imprisonment of their birth.

A year later in 1999, I was privileged to lead the first TIC Missions trip to visit Das and Doris and see the ministry first-hand. We stood on the ground that now houses the Grace Clinic and the Bindu Home. We heard that just six weeks earlier, a Mennonite nurse from Indiana who was Das's long-time friend from their Vietnam days, Grace Mishler had stood on the same ground and prayed that God might find a way to allow Das to build a health clinic for the children in the home to care for their malnutrition, childhood diseases, and snakebites.

We asked Das about how much money he needed to build such a health care facility. He told us in Indian Lakhs and when we converted that amount into Taiwan dollars, we realized to our amazement that we had raised and brought with us almost exactly that amount (about US$14,000) from the TIC congregation and from local Buddhist women who had a heart for the work that Pastor Das was doing in India. Providentially, the single biggest contribution came from a TIC parishioner named Grace Lee now living in Vancouver who met us on the morning of our departure from Taipei saying that God had been motivating her all week to take the money that she had saved over several years for her own master's degree and donate it to the health clinic in Mallepalli. Hence the naming of the Grace Clinic for the two "Graces" and the amazing grace of our Lord in working His will through these two women who never met each other.

[At that time, children in the Bindu Home were endangered by the poisonous snakes that came onto the school grounds. Once bitten, they had little chance to survive the three-hour journey to the nearest medical facility to get antidotes to combat the snake venom. Since then, the Lawrence family from TIC paid for a wall to be built completely around the school grounds that prevents snakes

and pigs and other wandering animals from coming onto the campus.]

Since that first visit in 1999, TIC has led or partici- pated in about nine mission trips that have taken on two distinct flavors: (1) Pastor's Seminars for the rural village pastors, missionaries and their spouses that Das's ministry supports and (2) Dental Clinics for the nearby villagers in Mallepalli and Deverkonda to allow the local Muslims and Hindus to understand the veracity of John 3:16, that "God so loved the world that He sent" . . . people like you and me to be witnesses to His great love for all persons of all races, genders, religions, and creeds.

Perhaps the most significant legacy of TIC's eleven- year relationship with the ministries of the Matilda Education Society (MES) is the birth of a half dozen partnerships between present and former members of TIC with MES that have taken on a life of their own. One ex- ample is Wayne Lawton, a retired U.S. schoolteacher, lay preacher and former member of TIC, after relocating back to the U.S., has returned several times to support Das by offering his physical labor and by providing rural village pastoral training in the church planting that Das has car- ried out in the region.

This narrative gives you a glimpse into the bridge of love that has been built between Taipei and the Matilda Education Society. Our witness has now expanded to Shanghai since Pastor Nathan Showalter and his wife Christina are now serving the Shanghai Abundant Grace International Fellowship attended by many former mem- bers of TIC whose companies or schools have moved them to China. This fellowship has already sent a work trip to rebuild homes on the tsunami-damaged seacoast and has collected funds to support the reconstruction of a church and the building of more homes.

We see the work continuing as Das, Doris, and son Nathan continue to serve the Lord and do His will among these communities in Andhra Pradesh.

Gerry Cooper was a member of the Taipei (Taiwan) International Church (TIC) Missions Committee and has coordinated a number of medical and dental mission trips from his congregation to India to assist Matilda schools, Bindu home children, and rural village pastors.

Dental Team Visit from Taipei

Robin Truslow, as told to David Janzen: September 2010

We are expatriates who came to Taiwan because my husband David has work here as an engineer. When our family arrived, we joined the Taipei International Church (TIC) and soon learned about the Bindu Home in India, run by Das and Doris Maddimadugu. Others in our congregation were sponsoring a Bindu child, so we did, too. It means a lot to our two girls.

About two years ago I was sitting in church, and week after week I'd hear announcements of this dental mission trip to India, asking for volunteers. I am the last person who'd ever go on a mission trip. I normally pick the hotels with the most stars. But I had this terrible nudging feeling from the Spirit that I should go, only I could excuse myself because I have no dental skills. And then one week, they asked if anyone could play the recorder because the Matilda school has a recorder choir and they needed some training help. Then I thought, "Oh, sister, make your plans. Now you have to go."

So we went and taught some new songs to the re-corder choir, left them some music books, and gave more advanced lessons to the teachers so they could train the children further. But much of the time I would be with the children while they waited for their dental care. After the initial exam, each child would get a colored card indicating what treatment they needed. After a while the children figured out that a red card meant an extraction, and tears would come rolling down their cheeks. So we'd hold them on our laps and try to comfort them.

At the end of the week I decided to sponsor another child. So Das brings me two children, a little boy and a girl and tells me their stories. Then he asks, "Which one do you want to sponsor?" Well, by that time my heart already had gone out to each of them, so I could not choose. I ended up sponsoring both of them. That evening at our group's farewell Das spoke about how generous I had been to sponsor two children. "Only now," he added, "I wish I'd shown her three." This was typical Das, giving thanks and credit, but also suggesting we might do more to meet the need. We all were captivated by this kind and giving couple whose example spreads to everyone around.

Then on the last day, an orphan girl with beautiful rings in her ears, comes up to me as we are leaving, takes off her earrings and gives them to me. I was overwhelmed. I think it was all she had. From pastor Das and Doris they have learned this spirit of love that is so amazing. I am so grateful for all we experienced in these ten days. It gave us such a boost in our love and walk with Jesus.

Robin Truslow, with her husband David and two girls, are members of the Taiwan International Church and sponsors of three Bindu Home children. In 2008 Robin was a member in the TIC dental mission to Mallepalli and Devarakonda.

A Housing Project for Tsunami Survivors

Following the Tsunami crisis of 2004 we helped oversee a project in Bapatla, on the Indian Ocean coast. In partnership with the Abundant Grace Church in Shanghai, China, we built twenty houses for families whose homes had been destroyed in the tidal wave. Following this project, Christians in the area began to meet in a house fellowship where we give encouragement and support to the pastor, Raja Rao. Since then we have built a prayer hall and many who were secret Christians are now gathering for worship.

Visiting Twenty Homes for Tsunami Victims

David Janzen: Journal

November 13, 2007: It was a six-hour drive from Mallepalli to the East Indian coast. We came to see a joint project between the Abundant Life Community Church of Shanghai and the Matilda Education Society to build twenty houses. Ten of them are completed and ten still need windows, plaster, and other finishing touches. We saw all of them in a village about two miles inland from the coast. These homes were all for fisherman families who had lived on the beach, but after surviving the Tsunami, they did not want to rebuild where a wave could catch them again.

They told us that the Tsunami came in the daytime, and the wave—while it was still far out at sea—was tall, loud, and terrifying. People ran from it, and most of them got caught in the onrushing water, but survived. They thanked God that only twenty-one died in the region. But all their homes and belongings were destroyed. In the first phase of relief, the Matilda Educational Society provided clothes, plates, cups, and utensils for several hundred families. Then Das, with Mennonite Central Committee resources, arranged to build thirty boats for the fishermen so they could regain their livelihoods. Now they are building houses. Of the twenty families getting homes, four are Christians, the rest Hindu and Muslim.

While going around the village with our entourage, I was impressed by Das's sensitivity and wisdom in so many areas. He remembers people's names and greets them, recalling previous conversations—women and children as well as the men who have responsibility for the housing project. Das asks if people want to pray, and they eagerly respond, gathering in a circle. I notice his habit of stepping out of his sandals for prayer. He keeps me in touch with translations and explanations. In his quiet patient way, he keeps track of everything important, consults with people as he goes to get their advice. He took the contractor along so he could see the whole context. Even though they are about $9,500 short of the funds needed, he tells the contractor to begin the last phase. "The rest of the money will come." They plan a dedication for all the houses for early 2008.

A Hindu Nationalist politician in black garb shadowed the group for a while and then made his speech, accusing the project of taking fifty applications and building only twenty houses. He is upset that the plaque at the entrance to the project does not mention him as a matter of protocol and respect. We hear him out. Das explains that M.E.S made pledges for only twenty houses and has never promised more than that. "When these twenty are finished, we can talk about others." Das responds in other words I don't understand. He asks the people around if what he says is right, and they say it is so. Then Das nods for his assistant Sherjeel to engage the man some more, which he does. Our group, including many village women and children, continued talking with the woman-owner of an almost-finished house After a while the Hindu politician shakes Sherjeel's hand, Das's hand, my hand, gets on his motorcycle and rides away. We all relax a bit.

While taking pictures of the houses, several women asked me to take their photos, too. When I showed them how they looked on the camera monitor, they were tickled no end and asked me to take more pictures, calling other friends into the frame. Very quickly I had four, five, six girlfriends. They were all giggles—looking at themselves in the camera. One with a red sari thanked me profusely in words I could not understand, and kissed my hand several times. I need to make prints and get them back somehow.

A part-time pastor named Matthew and his new wife Susanna are visiting the community regularly, and a growing group of Christians has been meeting in a house fellowship with them.

Torrential Rains

In 2009 torrential rains hit Andhra Pradesh submerging many villages and towns, and breaching manmade dams and reservoirs. Hundreds of people died or were missing. Efforts were made by government officials, but they were not prepared for this kind of deluge. Some of us pastors went to assess the loss of life, houses, and livestock. Pastor Raja Rao, in Bapatla, recommended that we undertake a relief effort in Repalle where he also pastors a church. We sent a team of five persons, including myself, and ten local volunteers to attend to the needs in Christian and humanitarian compassion. We distributed blankets, kitchen utensils, school textbooks, and school supplies for 500 families.

Chapter 6

Indigenous Ministry
and the Power of Weakness

Here to Stay in the Face of Whatever Comes

As an indigenous ministry, we are always reminded that we
are a minority people, a people with limited financial resources,
often depending on outside contributions. Not being attached
to a mission organization, we have no reserve funds from mission boards or foundations. This tempts us to waver in faith at
times. On the other hand, it leads us to depend more on God
than on our own strength. Most of our friends and some of their
churches continue to support us whole-heartedly, for which we
are thankful.

Being indigenous also means that we are not separate from
the local community when it comes to suffering and sharing our
faith. This makes it easy for us to be accepted or rejected since
we live among the people. Christianity in the region is not ex-
empt from caste consciousness, which divides humanity. But as
Christians, we seek to bind up the brokenness of society. Being
indigenous means that, unlike the overseas missionaries, we are
here to stay in the face of whatever may come.

We have had two decades of involvement in rural India by
sharing our simple faith, coupled with efforts to improve conditions of the poor. While our work has been under restraint,
we equally experience the joy and peace of the Lord because of

those restraints. In the process our lives have been thrown out of joint. Our daughters, living in the U.S. and Canada, have become strangers living in strange lands, while someone else's children became like our own. In all this, we extract a meaning for our lives as Christ's love binds us together in his service. We cannot ask for more than this.

Life Coming Full Circle?

David Janzen: Journal

November 17, 2007: This morning, Das and I visited the farm one last time. The golden rice we saw two days ago had been scythed and now lay in sheaves on the stubble, drying and ready to thresh in a few days. Soon it will feed Bindu Home children standing in straight rows with bowls in hand, singing their thanks to God before they eat.

When Das is on the farm he relaxes and recalls memories of his earlier life and what God has brought him through. I feel especially honored in going back with Das to his roots in the village of Angadipet and on the land that he and his brother have developed until his brother's death three years ago. When we are here, Das's soul seems at rest. He wonders if he and Doris might not be happy retiring to a little cabin on the farm when all his duties are in the hands of others. Here he would get a roto tiller and plow up the ground between his sweet lime trees, live simply, and receive only those visitors who cared to walk the mile from the highway and sit with him among his vegetables, sheep, fruit trees, and rice paddies.

This would describe a full circle of life—beginning in an obscure village among the untouchables with a blind father who could not support him, rescued from bonded labor by a single-woman missionary—Helen Warkentin, a good mission school education where he discovered his gift for learning, training as a medical lab technician, MCC service in Vietnam with Doris at his side, a few years of Bible training at Canadian Mennonite Bible College in Winnipeg, advanced education in the Overseas Ministry Study Center at Princeton Divinity School. A gifted and internationally connected man with a beautiful and resourceful wife—they could have gone anywhere in the world to thrive in comfortable professional service.

However, Das and Doris felt called back to India where he pastored an urban Mennonite Brethren congregation in Hyderabad for eight years while their three children grew up. A dream persisted that called him back to his people, to develop holistic ministries demonstrating the new way of living that Jesus brings. These ministries of presence and creativity have borne good fruit in many transformed lives and in institutions that show how Christians, tribal people, Hindus, and Muslims, can thrive together in integrity and peace.

I remember reading Eric Erickson's biography of Gandhi that recapitulates the five stages in the Indian understanding of a good life: the cycle includes childhood learning, marrying and becoming a householder, prospering, then pouring yourself into another generation so that they might become fruitful, and finally reaching the stage of simplicity that relinquishes responsibility and perfects the soul in contemplation. For Das and Doris this would mean ending up in a hut on the land, laboring with their own hands to grow food in stillness and close to God.

But I don't think Das will complete the circle because his body and health will not carry him that far, and his friends will keep on needing him, and God will continue to give him visions. The Biblical image for a fruitful old age is found in Joel 2 and in Acts 2 where God declares, "I will pour out my Spirit upon all flesh, and your sons and your daughters shall prophesy, your young men shall see visions, and your old men will dream dreams. Even upon my slaves, both men and women, I will pour out my Spirit; and they shall prophesy." The generations need each other to complete the dreams God gives them. I hope Das and Doris have many retreats on the farm in years to come, but I expect the visions and new initiatives to continue as long as God gives them life.

After Twenty-Two Years of Ministry in Nalagonda, We are Retiring But Not Quitting

May, 2011

Dear David and Joanne,

Twenty-two years ago you encouraged us to go ahead to start a ministry among my people in the Nalgonda region of Andhra Pradesh. Doris and I gradually moved from Hyderabad to Devarkonda as our children grew older. During this time we have seen God's hand at work and we acquired a network of praying and supporting partners for which we are most grateful.

About a year ago we prayed about relinquishing our roles of leadership and were moved to let the younger generation take responsibilities. Our son, Nathan Anand, and the Matilda board members have worked with us for several years to gain insight to manage the organizational affairs. There is a strong pastoral presence in the board members who are committed to the Lord's work. We know that the Lord will give them wisdom and direction to care for the Bindu Home, the schools in Devarakonda and Mallepalli, and the Grace Clinic. Other programs may need to be dropped.

We moved to Hyderabad last month, but we continue to travel back and forth to Mallepalli, mainly to keep in touch with the pastoral ministry of eighteen churches and the small farm at Angadipet which we nurtured for many years. Yesterday we let the final batch of rabbits go find a home with the person who cares for them.

Last week we attended two weddings one in Vijayawada and one in Mallepalli. The Mallepalli wedding was dear to us since the bride, a tribal woman raised in the Bindu home from her infant days, now has achieved a [university] scholarship to study in the department of horticulture.

This year's tenth-grade class results were encouraging. Three girls achieved merit ranks and another three girls scored 100/100 on their math exam, which gives them recognition on the state level. Nathan is proud of the class since there was a hundred percent success rate on the state exams. Our school is a witness to the society.

Now that we are no longer part of the school and Bindu Home administration, we do not want to live from the precious little contributions that come for the children and the work. We need an independent living. Since you asked, our monthly financial needs during retirement for food, travel, utilities, communications, pastoral seminars, and visiting churches will be about $866 a month or $10,363 a year. We would like to live on our own as long as possible. I will greatly appreciate if you prayerfully consider these needs. After you read this you may wish to share this information with our friends.

We are retiring but not quitting. Pray for us.

Love, Das and Doris

[The above is a composite of portions from several letters written in the month of May, 2011.]

Behold, I Do a New Thing

David Janzen: Journal

4-16-12: As this book moves on to the printers more can added about the shape of Doiris and Das's life beyond "retirement."

Doris has suffered increasing sciatic pain in her back and left leg. A doctor recommended surgery, but instead Das and Doris went to Bangalore where a spine specialist gave her daily massages for two weeks with the result that "Doris seems to be improving. She can bend her back easier than before and sleeps well through the night. The doctor says that her knee problem is related to a certain nerve in the base of the spine. Once the knot in the back is eased the knee will move freely".

Earlier this year, Dave Wilson, a pastor friend from the United Kingdom, came for a week of village preaching and support for pastors. "He took us through the Gospel of John explaining how God embraced this world with His infinite love and saving grace. Over 1,000 persons attended the meetings from eight villages in the region of Devarkonda. There was much jubilation in the night gatherings with singing and tribal dancing."

Das and Doris are now animated by a new vision, to build a Christian summer camp for pre-teens on an acre of land carved out of the family farm near Angadipet. Gerry Cooper and friends from the Taipei International Church are hoping to fund this construction of dormitories for about 70 children and homes for staff to lead them. Das and Doris want to live there, oversee the farm, and be surrounded by the teachers and children who will give their days meaning. As long as God gives them strength, they have no wish for an idle retirement.

Das writes: "I have retained the following responsibilities after my retirement in October 2011:

- Rural church new construction, repairs and completion of unfinished work,

- Pre-Teen camps,

- Pastoral seminars,

- Scholarship support for a two-year job-oriented skills program after 10th grade to keep me in contact with the spiritual ministry of the Matilda Education Society.

- Reorganizing our structures so that church work can be separate from educational and social responsibilities since our nationalist government is pushing for less freedom of non-profit organizations in the expression of Christian faith.

Finally, in looking back over the stories of this book, it strikes me how biblical they feel. With Das and Doris, we are somehow included in the lineage of Joseph in prison, Hannah the childless one pleading with God, David the last and least of the brothers, Mary and Joseph giving birth in a stable before fleeing as refugees from the wrath of Herod. God keeps using the nobodies of the world to show up the powers of this age, the broken ones to show God's strength, unlikely friendships arranged by the Spirit to redeem and give hope to this tired world, using even you who read this book to birth and sustain a new creation.

Any royalties from this book will be contributed to the work of Matilda Ministries and the monthly retirement-but-not-quitting expenses of Das and Doris. Your questions and contributions are welcome at:

Reba Place Church (for India Mission)
737 Reba Place Basement
Evanston IL 60202
dhjanzen@gmail.com

I Remember

Peter, Peter

Peter, Peter,
Why do you seek me
Among the dead?
Seek me
Among the living,
In the colonies
Of lepers, the blind
And the crippled.
Prepare a table
Among them.
I'll break bread
With them
Before I'm crucified
Once again.

—Das Maddimadugu